Contents

Introduction

Management is an important part of the role of both carer managers and child carers in all early years settings, as more children are cared for by external agencies. The book takes a look at management theory and explains how this can be applied to practice in the early years.

Learning begins at birth. The essential management task for the child carer and carer manager is to provide for the learning child. This requires knowledge and understanding of child development. This book stresses the emotional, social and intellectual development in particular, and demonstrates how understanding helps in the management of these needs.

Curriculum planning and assessment are important aspects of the learning process. The book provides concrete examples to illustrate how to manage the curriculum and assessment effectively.

The way a child learns is through exploring the environment. The book examines how the environment can be designed to be both stimulating and safe, and how it can support active learning.

Child care management includes the management of carers as well as management of children. Knowledge of management strategies will be a tool for a better interaction between the carer and the child and the carer manager and other carers.

This book is written especially for students studying for either the Advanced Diploma in Child Care and Education or the National Vocational Qualification (NVQ) Level 3 in Early Years Care and Education, who may be unfamiliar with but interested in management theory. It does not aim to be a training manual but rather a guide to the application of management theory. Management is the formal way of looking at what you do instinctively, which is caring for children.

Acknowledgements

I wish to thank Carolyn Meggitt for suggesting that I write this book, having confidence in my ability and smoothing the way for Anna Clark at Hodder & Stoughton to commission it. My thanks to Audrey Curtis for her guidance with the text and her encouragement. I am grateful to Alma Ramnauth, paediatric Nurse Tutor, for her constructive criticism especially on the Health aspects, and to Peter McComisky for his generous support and help on the management theories. Above all, I am indebted to Brenda Robb (Principal of the Vicarage Nursery School, London, SW14 and Partner in the Richmond upon Thames Early Years Scheme). Without her this book would not have been written and her contribution has been enormous. In particular, my thanks for her discussion with Eleanor Goldschmeid on 'Heuristic Play'. I was able to use her setting, the Vicarage Nursery, to acquire information on the practical side. My thanks also to the parents and the children of the Vicarage Nursery School for allowing me to use their pictures in the text. I wish to acknowledge the technical assistance from all my colleagues at college. Thank you for your patience. Thanks to my NVQ and ADCE students for giving me the inspiration.

Preface

Both internationally and nationally, governments and other organisations are highlighting the importance of offering good quality care and education to children under statutory school age. In the UK the government is committed to providing part-time nursery places for all 3 and 4-year-olds. At the same time, financial assistance is to be given towards child care costs for mothers in low paid jobs so that they can return to work

Increased provision is to be welcomed, but it must go hand in hand with high quality care and education and this means well trained staff who understand the needs of both children and adults in institutional settings. *Management in the Early Years* will help practitioners to meet those needs. It is one of the few books which clearly identifies the main issues involved in managing these settings. Verna Lyus has brought her wealth of knowledge and experience together to produce a highly readable book which addresses the major areas of concern. Each chapter looks at a specific aspect of management, and is supported by useful additional references, as well as activities to help students in their learning.

Quality care and education will only be achieved if all early years practitioners have a sound understanding of the needs of all those involved in early childhood settings. Management skills, which play an important part in this understanding, are often overlooked during initial professional training. Hopefully readers will find that this book will help them meet the challenge.

Audrey Curtis
May 1998

1

Child Care in Perspective

This chapter puts into context the reasons behind the need for professional and affordable child care. Statistics support the view that women are taking a more active part in the workplace as the number of part-time flexible jobs increases. Recent legislation defines the rights of all children and regulates child care provision.

Child care in the United Kingdom

Motherhood is no longer a full-time career for the majority of women in the UK. Most mothers today with children under the age of 18 have paid jobs outside the home and are no longer full-time carers of their children (*Social Trends*, 28).

In the UK the main providers of pre-school child care are:

▶ Relatives (spouse, grandparents) or friends
▶ Registered childminders
▶ Private day nurseries
▶ Nursery schools or playgroups
▶ Nannies
▶ Au pairs.

The nature and function of each of these providers are discussed in Chapter 4.

Some parents are able to adjust their worktime to be with their children so that there is at least one parent present all the time.

In some families, where the mother is the principal earner, the father assumes the role of the prime carer. In other families the mother works while the child is cared for by a non-family member. Where the natural parents are divorced, the child's carer may be a single parent. If parents remarry, children may be cared for by step-parents, step-sisters or brothers, or one of four sets of grandparents.

Since the 1980s women's role in society has changed as more women, especially mothers, have entered the labour force. For the foreseeable future, where both parents work, some form of child care will be the rule rather than the exception. Even women who choose to stay at home to bring up their children may make use of child care services such as playgroups.

Changing patterns of modern family life

The extended family

The family in the UK has traditionally been the most important provider of child care. Advances in technology and changes in industry, together with the growth of individualism and consumerism, have all had their effects on family life. The extended family of grandparents, aunts and other relatives, once a reliable source of child care, is no longer the norm. Families are separated by distance, time and changed relationships.

In contrast, although there are significant differences in family situations between the different ethnic groups in the UK, various studies suggest that to all of them the support of the extended family is very important. A study in Birmingham revealed that almost 9 in 10 Asian-born people in the sample had relatives living within 10 minutes walk, compared with 1 in 3 of the rest of the population.

According to the 1991 Census there are over three million people from ethnic minority groups living in the UK, representing 5.5 per cent of the total population. The table below shows how this percentage is made up.

Ethnic groups as a percentage of the total UK population

Ethnic group	% in UK population
Black groups: black Caribbean, black African, black other	1.6
South Asian groups: Indian, Pakistani, and Bangladeshi	2.7
Chinese and others	1.2

Source: 1991 Census

The nuclear family

The nuclear family that includes mother, father and 2.5 dependent children all living together has traditionally been seen as central to Western life. Since

1961 the number of nuclear families has been in decline. Recent figures show that only one household in four represents the 'traditional' nuclear family. On the other hand, the number of lone parent families has grown substantially (see the table below).

The increase in the number of lone parent families in the UK, 1972–96 (in millions)

United Kingdom	1972	1981	1986	1992	1996
Couple with					
1 child	16	18	18	17	6
2 children	35	41	28	37	38
3 or more children	41	29	28	28	26
Lone mother					
1 child	2	3	4	5	5
2 children	2	4	5	7	7
3 or more children	2	3	3	6	6
Lone father					
1 child	–	1	1	–	1
2 children	1	1	1	1	1

Source: *General Household Survey*, Office for National Statistics

The female heads most lone parent families. The traditional matriarchal arrangement found in lone parent families in the Caribbean is now the pattern among these families in the UK. In the 1991 Census, there were just over 4 in 10 black families with lone parents, compared to 1 in 8 white families and 1 in 10 south Asian families. Women are no longer necessarily living in nuclear families dependent upon a stable relationship with a male breadwinner.

Women are now able to choose whether or not to have children, when to have them and how many. In 1991, a survey projected that approximately 20 per cent of British women born between 1960 and 1980 would remain childless (Dunnell, K. 1976).

The parent and the need to work

If there was enough money 8 out of 10 men would stay at home. 8 out of 10 women would choose part-time work.

(Guardian 27 June 1996)

Historically, in most cultures, child care has been women's work. In the UK of the 1990s, the role of women is being transformed. More women are filling part-time, temporary and seasonal jobs, and the focus of women's work is shifting from the home to the workplace. In contrast, more men are currently unemployed and at home while their partner works.

In 1971, women made up 38 per cent of the workforce compared with 44 per cent in 1997. This number is expected to rise to 50 per cent by the year 2006. The labour force statistics shown below slightly overstate the increase for men and understate the increase for women. This is partly due to the change in definition of unemployment as used by the former civilian labour

Labour force by gender and age in the UK from 1971 to the projection for 2006

United Kingdom		Millions			
	16–24	25–44	45–54	55–59	all over 16
Males					
1971	3.0	6.5	3.2	1.5	16.0
1981	3.2	7.1	3.0	1.4	16.0
1991	3.1	8.1	3.0	1.1	16.4
1997	2.4	8.1	3.4	1.1	16.0
2001	2.4	8.2	3.4	1.3	16.3
2006	2.6	7.8	3.5	1.4	16.4
Females					
1971	2.3	3.5	2.1	0.9	10.0
1981	2.7	4.6	2.1	0.9	10.9
1991	2.6	6.1	2.4	0.8	12.4
1997	2.0	6.4	2.9	0.8	12.7
2001	2.1	6.4	3.0	0.9	13.1
2006	2.2	6.4	3.2	1.1	13.6

Source: *Social Trends 28* (1998) Office for National Statistics London, page 75.

force to produce the figures for 1971 and 1981; in later years the International Labour Organisation (ILO) definition has been used and members of the armed forces are not included.

Compared with our European neighbours, the UK has the most women in paid work with the exception of Germany. Surveys (*Social Trends*, 27) have shown that 67 per cent of women in the UK with children under the age of 10 are in part-time work compared to 55 per cent of women with older children. Statistically, an even higher percentage of women with older children work full-time.

The increase in the number of women in part-time work is partly due to the changing nature of employment. There is a greater demand by employers for professional and nonprofessional, flexible, part-time workers. The change in employment patterns and gender roles allows women greater participation in the workplace. Women are far more likely to be part-time employees: 45 per cent of female employees, but only 8 per cent of male employees, were working part-time in Spring 1996. The gender gap in employment is narrowing, but partly as a result of men's deteriorating employment position. The difference in employment trends between men and women is the result of the over-representation of women in most forms of part-time jobs, temporary contracts, homeworking, and so on.

There is a trend towards professional women choosing a career first, giving birth at an older age and then returning to work more quickly. Continuous employment careers are becoming more common within this group. Research carried out by the Policy Studies Institute reveals that two out of three women return to work after giving birth. In 1996, on average, mothers took 27 weeks' maternity leave, but 14 per cent of women who were entitled to the statutory minimum of 14 weeks took less than that amount; it is unclear whether this was due to financial pressure or the reluctance to interrupt careers. The need for child care provision has grown as women have sought to juggle their working lives with family responsibilities. Women in full-time employment still see their families as their first responsibility. While mothers have become increasingly involved in the labour force research shows that, in contrast, fathers' contribution to domestic life has not increased proportionately (Brannen and Moss, 1991).

Father as main carer

One recent study found, however, that, in general, the more mothers were involved with work outside the home, the more fathers shared equally in child care (*Social Policy Research*, 1996). In the same study, over one third of mothers named fathers as providers of child care, regardless of the age of the children involved. Working fathers either alone or in partnership with other care sources, provided care in 40 per cent of cases where the child was aged under five and in 50 per cent of situations where the child was over five (Ferri and Smith, 1996).

Men, through circumstances such as unemployment, may find themselves in the role of nurturer rather than provider. Ferri and Smith found that in families where only the mother was employed 75 per cent of fathers were involved with child care. Paradoxically, unemployed fathers figured as sole carers in just 39 per cent of cases where children were of pre-school age and in 50 per cent of cases where children were over five years of age. Statistically, fathers who were unemployed did not make a significantly greater contribution to child care than those in employment, even when their partners worked. Compared with other European countries, men in the UK work the longest hours away from home. The above survey concluded that where men work over 50 hours per week, their contribution drops sharply regardless of their partner's employment situation.

The findings of Ferri and Smith's survey suggest that fathers are not adapting easily to their new caring roles. Those fathers least involved in caring for their children appear to be most satisfied with their lives while those most involved in child care were least satisfied, particularly when they also worked long hours. It seems that although fathers may be spending more time with their children they are still not providing emotional support: years of working unsociable hours may mean that the father has no previous practical experience in child care and for some unemployed men the perceived role demotion causes resentment. Many fathers, however, are grateful for the opportunity to develop the nurturing side of their characters and actively enjoy spending time with their families.

Child care for children under five

In the UK, there are 3.8 million children of four years old and under, almost seven per cent of the population. Almost six in ten families have at least one child under the age of five years. Nearly two thirds of mothers with children under five use some additional form of care for their children (see the table opposite).

Whereas in 1980, 80 per cent of parents relied on relatives to help with child care, today 50 per cent **have** to use professional child care services.

Child care provision for children under five, UK, 1991

Type of care	% of families with children 0–4 years
Unpaid family or friends	25%
School/nursery school	25%
private/voluntary schemes	17%
paid childminder/nanny	11%
Local authority scheme	7%
Workplace facility	1%
Total Using Care	**64%**

(Note: percentages add to more than the total because some respondents use more than one form of care)

Source: General Household Survey 1993, Office for National Statistics

A child arriving at nursery is welcomed by a carer

Child care policy

As governments change, policies change. Government policy on providing funds for child care also changes. After World War II politicians promoted full-time motherhood as the appropriate role for women (perhaps with population increase in mind). Women's wartime jobs were sacrificed in order to create room in the workplace for returning soldiers. With women returning to child care, the government could save money on nursery provision. Women have struggled to regain their role in the workplace, and today even those who can afford to stay at home do not necessarily want to be full-time mothers.

Governments have come a long way but as yet there is no national strategy for the provision of child care. Such provision is more important now than ever before. The European Child Care Network's figures forecast that 60 per cent of women (not only mothers) in the UK would be working by 1995. In addition, they suggested that the demand for day-care in the European Union would increase over time. Even without any additional measures to assist with child care, labour force participation rates among women and their share of the labour force are expected to rise.

Demand will also increase because the available supply of alternative sources of child care (for example, relatives and other women caring for children in their own homes or in the child's home) will decrease as more women enter the labour market. Reports highlight the increasing cost of child care. In 1993 figures showed that it cost between £50,000 and £80,000 to bring up a child in Britain, if the cost of child care is included. Today those figures are twice as much. Without the cost of child care, the average spending on children from birth to 17 years is slightly over £50,000. (*Social Policy Research*, 1997). Working mothers are spending almost twice as much on child care as on housing or food bills. The Day Care Trust findings reveal that only 25 per cent of working mothers can afford to pay for full-time child care while more than 45 per cent have to rely on informal and unregulated child care provided by relatives, friends or babysitters.

In the UK, unlike many other European countries, child care is not subsidised. Nevertheless, as an issue it is moving up the political agenda. In 1997, the government committed itself to a National Child Care policy. It continues to fund part-time education places for all eligible 4-year-olds and plans to extend this provision to all 3-year-olds. In addition, the government is using lottery money to fund after-school clubs. However, the provision of two and a half hours 'educare' per day for 3 and 4-year-olds and the possibility of three hours of after-school supervision is inappropriate to the care requirements of most working parents.

The concept of childhood

In the twentieth century, children have emerged as individuals with rights of their own. There was no concept of childhood in Europe until about the seventeenth century. If children survived infancy they were considered adults. Children wore adult clothes, were included in adult pastimes and were sent to work at the age of seven or younger (Brooks, J. 1987).

During the seventeenth century, with a decrease in infant mortality, families became closer and more concerned about their children's physical survival. However, until the end of the nineteenth century, children were punished without recourse because the prevalent belief was that children's moral states needed to be formed by strict correction. Adults measured themselves as effective parents through their success as reformers; the rights of the child were not considered in law until the twentieth century.

The rights of the child

The United Nations Convention on the Rights of the Child was put forward in 1989 and became international law on 2 September 1990. It was ratified by 187 of the United Nations member countries. The convention confirms the freedom a child needs to develop his or her intellectual, moral and spiritual capacities and demands, among other things, education, a healthy and safe environment, and minimum standards of food, clothing and shelter. The convention forms the basis of British child care legislation and informs policy. In general, the convention seeks to ensure that:

▶ the child's basic needs are met;
▶ the child is protected from cruelty and exploitation;
▶ parents are in a position to care properly and to the best of their ability for their children's needs;
▶ particularly vulnerable children, including those who cannot be with their families for whatever reason, receive the best possible care;
▶ children are given appropriate opportunities to play an active role in society and to have a say in their own lives.

The Children Act 1989

At a national level, British governments have always held the view that child care provision should be primarily a matter between parents and private and voluntary organisations. However, to ensure that day-care is of suitable quality the 1989 Children Act sets out the legislative and quality assurance framework for all service provision for children up to the age of eight.

The aim of the Act is to clarify the law relating to children. The Act seeks to achieve a balance between realistic regulation and growth in provision of services for the increasing number of children who need day-care. It requires local authorities to review and amend their child care policies, procedures and provision. The Children Act 1989 supersedes the many existing pieces of legislation previously accumulated in a piecemeal fashion over the years. The Act is a major piece of legislation and all those working in childcare **must** be familiar with its requirements.

It requires local authorities to:

▶ register day care providers, e.g. playgroups, childminders, nurseries, and to monitor the quality of childcare in these areas;
▶ ensure that children identified as having 'special needs' can go to a nursery, playgroup, after-school club or playscheme;
▶ inspect full-time and part-time day-care premises at least once every year;
▶ review, under Section 19 of the Act, the services in their area, listen to what people think about them and publish a report;
▶ assess under Part iii of the Act, the need for provision in their area of services and consult with various bodies in planning how that need will be met – the resulting plan must be published;
▶ ensure that, in court cases involving children, a child's welfare is the court's paramount consideration.

FIT PERSON

The Act also makes clear the notion of a 'Fit Person' to look after children:

> Where a person is proposing to look after children under eight, the social services department of the local authority has to be satisfied that he is 'fit' – i.e. suitable to do this . . . The local authority should have regard to these points when considering whether someone is fit to look after children under eight.

These points are:

▶ previous experience of looking after or working with young children or people with disabilities or the elderly;
▶ qualification and/or training in a relevant field such as child care, early years education, health visiting, nursing or other caring activities;
▶ ability to provide warm and consistent care;

▶ knowledge of and attitude to multi-cultural issues and people of different racial origins;

▶ commitment and knowledge to treat all children as individuals and with equal concern;

▶ physical health;

▶ mental stability, integrity and flexibility;

▶ no known involvement in criminal cases involving abuse to children.

ACTIVITIES

After reading the chapter you may like to complete some of the following activities:

1. IDENTIFY YOUR PERSONAL AND PROFESSIONAL ATTITUDE TOWARDS WORKING MOTHERS.

▶ How do you feel about mothers who go back to full-time work after their maternity leave?

▶ Do you have any experience as a working mother?

▶ Are the nursery sessions in your nursery timetabled for the convenience of commuters or shift workers?

2. WHAT MEASURES CAN BE TAKEN IN YOUR SETTING TO ENGAGE FATHERS MORE IN THEIR PARENTING ROLE?

▶ Do you actively try to recruit male staff?

▶ Do you treat fathers differently from mothers?

3. THE CHILDREN ACT 1989

Refer to the previous page. The Children Act sets out the points that a local authority is required to satisfy when considering whether a person is 'fit' to care for children under eight, including knowledge of and attitude to **multi-cultural** issues and people of different racial origins; commitment and knowledge to treat all children as individuals and with **equal concern**.

As a manager, think about these two issues and write down your thoughts as to the meaning of the phrases in relation to:

▶ How you relate to the children

▶ How you relate to your staff

▶ How you relate to the parents

▶ What are the implications for your practice.

If possible, share your findings with a colleague or fellow student.

Useful addresses

Carers National Association
20–25 Glasshouse Yard
London EC1A 4JS
Tel 0171 490 8818

The Daycare Trust
4 Wild Court
London WC2B 4AU
Tel 0171 405 5617

Commission for Racial Equality
Elliot House
Allington Street
London SW1E 5EF
Tel 0171 828 7022

Early Years Trainers Anti-Racist Network
(EYTARN)
PO Box 28, Wallasey
Merseyside L45 9N

Family Policy Studies Centre
231 Baker Street
London NW1 6XE
Tel 0171 486 8211

National Council for One Parent Families
255 Kentish Town Road
London NW5 2LX
Tel 0171 267 1361

Working for Childcare
77 Holloway Road
London N7 8JZ
Tel 0171 700 0281

Working Group Against Racism in Children's Resources
(WGARCR)
460 Wandsworth Road
London SW8 3LK

References

Brannen, J. and Moss, P. (1991) *Managing Mothers: dual earner households after maternity leave.* London: Macmillan.

Brooks, J. (1987) *The Process of Parenting.* London: Mayfield

Dormor, D. (1992) *The Relationship Revolution.* London: One Plus One.

Dunnell, K. (1976) *Family Formation Survey.* London: OPCS

Family Policy Studies Centre: *Family Policy Bulletin.* 1994, 1995, 1996, 1997.

Ferri, E. and Smith, K. (1996) *Parenting in the 1990s.* London: Family Policy Studies Centre.

Social Policy Research. 1995, 1996 and 1997 York: Joseph Rowntree Foundation.

Social Trends 28 (1988) Office for National Statistics, London.

Further reading

Joshi, H. (1989) *The Changing Population of Britain*. Oxford: B. Blackwell.

Twigg, J. (1992) *Carer: Research and Practice*. London: HMSO.

HMSO (1993) *General Household Survey* 1991, 1992 and 1994.

White, Carr and Lowe (1990) *A Guide to The Children Act 1989*. London: Butterworths.

Willmott, P. (1986) *Social Networks, Informal Care and Public Policy*. London: Policy Studies Institute.

2

A Management Model

There is a management element in all forms of child care. Essential to this chapter is understanding the distinction between the use of the terms **child carer** and **carer manager**. The child carer manages children. The carer manager manages both children and child carers at the same time. Throughout the book both terms are used. Nannies, au pairs and child minders fall into the first category, i.e. child carers. Nursery managers and playgroup leaders come into the second category, i.e. carer managers. A management model used in a child care setting can be applied to many situations from planning a programme to receiving quality ratings in external inspections. Each of the elements of the model used here: Planning, Organising Leading and Controlling, is applied within the context of child care from the point of view of a child carer and a carer manager.

Introduction to management

As a carer manager, you need to be familiar with a working model of management. Many practising managers define management as the act of getting things done through others. Formal management theory has its origins in the Industrial Revolution: the development of the steam engine brought about mechanised production in factories and the need to coordinate the tasks of factory workers and maximise resources to improve production created the role of the professional manager. With the developing complexity of industry there then arose the need for analysis of management difficulties. This led to the evolution of management theory.

Schools of thought on management theory

A school of thought reflects a definite point of view characterised by the problem studied, the method of study and the theories developed. Early contributors to management theory were scholars and practitioners who wrote about their subject and sought to generalise in order to develop basic principles. The foundation for most of their writing on management came from the fields of mathematics, engineering, economics, philosophy, psychology, military strategy and political science.

Among the various schools of management thought are:

▶ The Classical School
▶ The Human Relations School.

THE CLASSICAL SCHOOL OR SCIENTIFIC MANAGEMENT

Frederick W. Taylor (1856–1971) is regarded as the 'father' of 'scientific management'. His findings are described as a set of principles rather than a comprehensive theory. He argued that management ought to be based on sound, well-defined principles rather than depending on obscure ideas. His famous four principles of scientific management were:

▶ The development of a true science of work.
▶ The scientific selection and progressive development of workmen.
▶ The bringing together of the science and the scientifically selected and trained men.
▶ The constant and intimate cooperation between management and workers.

Taylor was interested primarily in increasing productivity on the shop floor. In scientific management the individual worker lost ownership of the knowledge unique to his craft: as a worker's skill was subjected to systematic analysis, the responsibility for planning work processes could be taken over by management. The Human Relations School developed as a reaction to the de-humanising nature of scientific management. It emphasised the significance of human relationships in the workplace.

THE HUMAN RELATIONS SCHOOL

The Human Relations School is the most relevant to child care management because it draws from the psychology of human behaviour and emphasises social factors such as:

▶ leadership style;
▶ motivation;
▶ interpersonal and organisational communication;
▶ staff morale;
▶ group cooperation;
▶ job satisfaction.

The major researchers contributing to the Human Relations School are Elton Mayo (1945), P. Drucker (1954), Abraham Maslow (1954) and Douglas McGregor (1960).

There is no single unified theory of management that can be applied successfully to all situations. However the following pattern is the core of all competent management. The process of **effective** management involves the ability to: **P**lan, **O**rganise, **L**ead and **C**ontrol.

The POLC model of management

▶ PLANNING   deciding what to do;
▶ ORGANISING   deciding how to do it;
▶ LEADING   directing how it is done;
▶ CONTROLLING   assessing and monitoring quality and informing new planning.

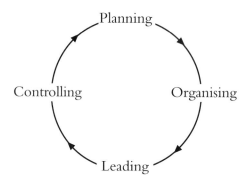

The carer manager's cycle of management

Task	Objectives		
Planning deciding what to do	to develop:	a	mission statement – strategic plan
		b	external and internal environment
		c	goals for workplace
		d	curriculum
Organising deciding how to do it	to organise:	a	manpower – staff and children
		b	materials and resources
		c	minutes – long, medium, short term plans
		d	money – income and expenditure
Leading directing how it is done	to support:	a	positive learning experiences
		b	motivation
		c	appropriate behaviour
		d	staff development
		e	staff during the inspection process
Controlling monitoring quality	to evaluate:	a	effectiveness of learning programme
		b	children's progress
		c	staff performance
		d	use of resources including partnership with parents

Management cannot be reduced to a simple checklist of activities as it is a process. The process of management involves a **systematic** and **organised** way of doing things. The key to successful management is understanding this process as a cycle of inter-related tasks. All child carers and carer managers, regardless of their workplace (playgroup, nursery, under five's centre) could use the POLC cycle to manage. You should approach the process with preset objectives in mind and the flexibility to adapt to unforeseen situations, which will arise in child care. The chart opposite shows some examples of objectives connected to each stage of the process. In child care we must insist that managing without putting the needs of every child at the **centre** of the process is ineffective.

Planning

Planning is concerned with what has to be done and how it should be done. Planning can be divided into **strategic** and **tactical** approaches.

Strategic planning

Strategic planning is a complex process, based on the objectives of the organisation and the allocation of resources to achieve those objectives. Strategic planning has to have a certain amount of flexibility to cope with 'what if' situations. There is always an element in any plan to allow for the contingencies of what might or might not happen. Strategic planning involves policy formulation and the development of a set of plans over a period of time, taking into consideration possibilities for expansion or contraction. In addition personnel, market opportunities and technological change all have to be considered.

EXAMPLE

If you wish to open a playgroup, you need to think beyond the day to day care of the children. You need to establish that a market exists, and plan how much the entire operation (buildings, staff salaries, resources, etc.) is going to cost.

The starting point for an organisation's strategic planning is the **mission statement**. The mission statement, widely used in industry, makes the purpose of the organisation clear. The underlying value system of an organisation is implicit in its mission statement which must provide answers to two questions:

▶ What is our business?
▶ What should it be?

In child care the basis of the mission statement must be the balance between care and education.

EXAMPLE

Sally, Tom, Zak and Lee, all with birthdays in the autumn, joined your playgroup in the term in which they turned three years. The children will be in the playgroup for six terms before they enter mainstream education as rising five year olds. It is clear that planning is essential if each child is to achieve the required learning goals by that stage. You are both helping the child to develop and preparing the child for school. Your strategic planning defines the end result you want for the children after being in a pre-school system, whether the child is at a playgroup or nursery.

The first step in the strategic planning process is to **identify**, **examine** and **plan** the goals for each child. The School Curriculum and Assessment Authority (SCAA) has specified the 'Desirable Outcomes for Children's Learning' (see Chapter 5) in the areas of:

▶ Personal and Social Development
▶ Language and Literacy
▶ Mathematics
▶ Knowledge and Understanding of the World
▶ Physical Development
▶ Creative Development.

In the case of the three children in the example above the long term or strategic plan must be that they maximise their potential and in the process move towards the desirable outcomes in all six areas of learning.

Tactical planning

This concerns the everyday activities necessary to achieve strategic goals. Tactical planning is short-term planning: the actual day to day implementation of the activities for the pre-school group. Tactical planning deals with the immediate future; in this context the educational timetable. The 'Desirable Outcomes for Children's Learning' will provide you with some of your objectives. You will also have objectives of your own stemming from the needs of the individual children.

Tactical planning will also involve relationships with parents, with the schools, inspectors, social workers and other external agencies.

Organising

Plans have to be made for the organisation of the **4Ms**.

	Examples
Materials	– what is the nature of the environment, what are your physical resources?
Manpower	– will you be operating entirely on your own or with staff?
Money	– this directly influences the availability of materials and manpower
Minutes	– time, how much time have you got?

Organising very much depends on the type of setting you manage. Each setting will have different requirements. There are differences between a playgroup, nursery school and childminder's home involving:

▶ the number of staff;
▶ the role of the staff;
▶ space allocation;
▶ the number of children.

Materials

The term 'materials' describes the physical aspect of the job – the location in terms of usage, space, environment, heating. What material resources do you have to achieve your plan? As carer manager, you will have overall responsibility for equipment, resources and materials. Basic resources or permanent areas of provision should be accessible to children to allow them to progress toward the 'Desirable Outcomes for Children's Learning'. A checklist of basic resources is given on page 84.

It is useful, where possible, to allocate separate storage areas to equipment and materials related to individual areas of learning, so that your staff may easily locate the resources needed to move children on to the next step in their learning.

You will need to provide additional materials related to topics and themes resulting from your medium and short-term planning.

These materials should:

▶ be matched to the task
   for example for junk modelling a variety of joining materials should be provided including PVA glue, Pritt Stick, Blue Tac, masking tape, sellotape and staplers.
▶ relate to children's current interest, enthusiasm, seasonal or community events
   for example if Divali is being celebrated materials to make a Rangoli might include flour, coloured sand, coloured rice and glitter.
▶ support learning priorities identified by ongoing observation
   for example if a child needs practice with recognising and recreating patterns, coloured beads, coloured bricks, tessellations or lego are some of the materials that can be used.
▶ be renewed frequently: a surprise a day is a good motto
   for example a 'surprise' rota may be set up to give each child the opportunity to bring in something special. This could be as simple as an interesting leaf or a bug in a jam jar.

Some materials must provide children with open-ended experiences, that is they allow children to experiment, to use materials in new ways, to explore possibilities, to enjoy the process as well as the end product.

Play equipment and materials should be of good quality, clean, well maintained and attractively presented to encourage children to select them. There should be a wide variety of equipment within each area of learning that will provide a range of challenges.

Manpower

'Manpower' is staffing. The adults with whom children have contact are their most important source of learning. Depending on your setting, you may conduct child care entirely on your own. If you are in a nursery or playgroup, however, it will be your responsibility to employ staff. This will involve careful selection and recruitment (see page 130). It is your task, as carer manager in a playgroup or nursery to ensure that you utilise your staff to the children's greatest benefit. You will begin by planning as a group, discussing and pooling ideas. Staff will need to identify what they hope children will learn in the long, medium and short term. They will work as a team to present learning to children in a coherent way. In deploying your staff, it is your responsibility to capitalise on individual strengths, interests and skills. It is important to maintain the correct balance between child-initiated and adult-directed activities.

Money

You need to ask yourself:

▶ Can you afford your provision?
▶ What are your costs?
▶ How is each child going to be funded?
▶ What financial records are needed?

The above questions have to be considered if effective management is to take place. The professional management of child care requires business skills. Whether childminder, playgroup manager or nursery manager, understanding the financial aspect of care and organising the effective use and control of your finances will be crucial to your survival as a business.

CAN YOU AFFORD YOUR PROVISION?

All carer managers agree that child care is expensive to provide. Therefore, you will need to look carefully at what you wish to provide and establish the

---

EXAMPLE

A break-even point

Outgoings (1997)	
Manager	£9,500
3 Nursery Assistants (part-time at £3,250 per annum)	£9,750
Rent (at £4.50 per hour)	£2,000
Food	£4,000
Medical and toiletries	£50
Replacement of equipment and furniture	£1,500
Consumable resources (paper, paint, etc.)	£1,500
Insurance	£500
Staff training	£1,500
Advertising	£210
Association fees	£100
Inspection fee	£12
Bank charges	£60
Subscriptions	£100
Telephone	£400
Total	**£22,132**
Total per child per year	**£1,318**
Total per child per term	**£439.33**

immediate and long-term costs of every aspect of that provision. You will need to identify your break–even point. This is the point at which you have sufficient money coming in from grants, fees, charities, to cover your overheads of rates, rent, heating, lighting and salaries if applicable. Calculating your break–even point will give you a clear indication as to whether you can afford your provision. An example is shown on the previous page.

Working capital

This is the sum of money you will need in the period between paying out for equipment, furniture, or materials and receiving fees from the parent. Your working capital should be included in the money that you have allocated to set up the provision. If you are unable to finance your project then money can be raised from a variety of sources – banks, charities, the Training and Enterprise Council. Each of these organisations will need to see on paper how you have thought through the workings of your business in terms of cash flow requirements. This is best presented in the form of a business plan. Preparing a business plan takes time but it is a useful tool to help you think through the potential for success or failure. Business plans may vary in length and attention to detail but they all follow a standard format (see Appendix 1).

What are your costs?

▶ Starting up costs
These are the initial one-off expenses that you have to meet to set up your home playgroup, or nursery.

Starting up costs

	Premises	Legal costs	Marketing costs	Equipment costs
Childminder	own home	none	none	low
Playgroup	rented hall, library	none	low	medium
Nursery	leasehold or freehold	yes	medium	high

▶ Staff costs

Staff salaries and National Insurance (NI) contributions

	Staff employed	**Cost**	**NI contributions**
Childminder	sole member	salary	yes
Playgroup	part-time staff. The number employed depends on size of playgroup	salary	yes
Nursery	full time and part time	salary	yes

HOW WILL CHILDREN BE FUNDED?

Fees are paid either by parents, family, Social Services or the Local Education Authority.

Childminders need to make formal billing arrangements with parents. Invoices should state when payment is due, to facilitate cash flow management.

Social Services funding must be applied for each term and the whole amount is paid directly to the provider shortly after the application has been approved.

The LEA grant is paid termly in two instalments as outlined in DfEE guidelines in *Early Years Development Partnership and Plans.*

▶ An interim payment of 50 per cent of grant due will be made at the beginning of each term, and will be based on the estimate of the number of children for whom the Plan provides.
▶ A balancing payment is made in the second half of the term once the LEA has received the results of the head count of eligible children receiving nursery education from registered providers (DfEE, 1988).

WHAT RECORDS ARE NEEDED?

Good accurate records are very important as they enable you to remain in control of your finances. They also reduce the time required by your accountant to prepare the accounts and thus save you money. If you are a childminder or playgroup manager you are not required to be audited. However if you receive government funding in payment for children's education you may be audited. The only requirements for the self-employed are that Income Tax returns and self-assessment forms have to be completed.

The accounting period for each financial year begins on 5 April.

You will need:

▶ Cash receipt book – for cash you have received from fees, grants, fundraising.
▶ Cash payment book – payments which you make for salaries, rent, utilities.
▶ Purchase book – to record, for example, materials, educational items purchased.
▶ Cheque books.
▶ Paying-in book.
▶ Bank statement file.

Minutes

Managing minutes relates to managing manpower to ensure that the best use is made of staff time and that there is non-contact time for meetings, planning and staff development. The carer manager must plan time wisely to ensure that staff work effectively as a team. There must be dedicated time for ongoing staff training and development. The management of time is directly related to curriculum planning: your timetable, your balanced programme to achieve your tactical plan for work and play.

As a carer manager you are challenged by SCAA to plan for effective use of time. This involves planning for long-term (across a year), medium-term (across a term) and short-term (day to day) provision. These plans must identify what staff intend to teach in each area of learning and how they will effect this teaching. The plans must also reflect what individual children can be expected to learn. Time must be allowed for assessment of children and evaluation of the learning programme. This aspect of managing minutes is dealt with in greater detail in Chapter 5.

Time must also be allocated for putting partnership with parents into practice.

EXAMPLE

Time must be set aside for correspondence with parents. The first contact a prospective parent has with a setting may be through the group's brochure, sent with a welcoming letter. Registration forms may have to be posted and receipt of deposits and fees acknowledged. There may be a regular newsletter to parents to be written.

It is important, however, not to swamp parents with written information. Sometimes, a notice on the board or a brief conversation is preferable. Time must also be allocated for visits. Carers may like to make a home visit before a child joins the group. There will also be pre-entry visits by the child and parents to the group.

Mutually convenient times will need to be found for parents and carers to meet to discuss individual children's progress. Social events will need to be arranged, such as coffee mornings, which enable parents to meet one another.

For the sake of clarity we have examined separately the above four aspects of organising: Material, Manpower, Money and Minutes. However all four overlap.

EXAMPLE

You need to buy a new piece of outdoor equipment (Materials) so staff (Manpower) have to meet after the session (Minutes) to choose between several options. You will have to pay staff extra (Money) for this additional meeting in keeping with good business practice.

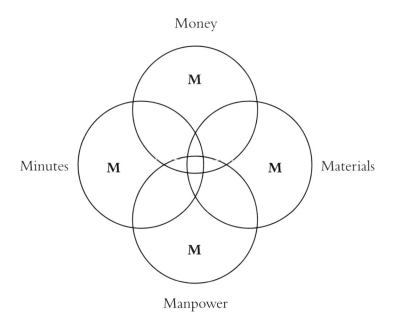

Money

Minutes   M   M   Materials

Manpower

What sort of organiser are you?

It is helpful to consider the sort of organiser you are.

▶ Is the **task** or the **child** more important?
▶ Are you a **task** or **people** organiser?

The **people person** looks at the provision from the child's point of view, whereas the **task person** focuses on the functional nature of the provision:

▶ The task person would say: 'We only have so much time and so many resources, but let's use the time usefully'.
▶ The people person would say: 'We only have so much time and so many resources but let's use the money we have got to cater for the children's needs'.

The process of planning and organising will achieve nothing unless you have the ability to put it into effect. You will have to motivate other carers, parents, volunteers, in such a way that they are willing to work individually and as a team to achieve the common purpose. In other words you must lead them.

Leading

The process of leadership

Leadership is the ability to influence the thoughts and behaviour of others so that they are willing to follow you. You are striving to get other people to do something you want them to do. Leadership is **not** the same as management. A person can be a leader without being a manager. In cricket, for example the captain is not the manager. He influences the behaviour of the team and is respected because of his superior skills. He decides how the fielding will be ordered on the day, but he does not have the responsibility to plan, organise or control where the matches will be played or against which team. This is the responsibility of the manager. Managers have the right to influence because of their position but they may not choose to use this right and in some cases managers may not have total power.

Leadership concerns working with people as individuals and in groups. The process of leadership entails a balancing of the needs of three key elements:

▶ Task
▶ Team
▶ Individual.

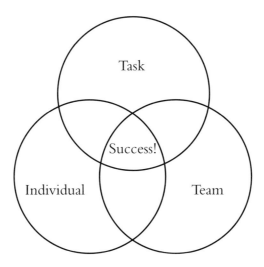

You will notice from the above figure that the three circles used to represent the three key elements overlap. This is because any particular action by you may satisfy more than one element. Conversely, at some point you may focus on any one aspect, to the partial exclusion of the others. For example you may be concentrating on getting all the paper work prepared for an inspection without realising that your team are experiencing fear and anxiety. The child carer may be concentrating more on completing an activity than attending to the needs of a child. However, through experience you will know that attention is essential to all three elements: the task, team and individual. Otherwise balanced leadership will not be taking place. As the leader, you need to consider the following:

THE TASK

You need to:

- ▶ be clear what the task is;
- ▶ know how it fits into the short and long-term planning;
- ▶ plan how to do it;
- ▶ provide resources, time and guidance;
- ▶ delegate to give you time for other things;
- ▶ ensure that the rules do not hinder the task;
- ▶ monitor and control the task;
- ▶ evaluate results.

THE TEAM

A team may develop from groups but unlike groups they are more cohesive. 'A team is a small number of people with complementary skills, who are committed to a common purpose, performance, goals and approach for which they hold themselves mutually accountable.' (Katzenbach and Smith, 1994). In a child care setting a team does have commitment to a shared purpose or goal and can provide a position of strength to support core values. However, if as a leader you lose your identity and individuality to the group you will over identify with what the group thinks and feels, going along with whatever the team thinks is best. The team is leading you. Your role is to lead and represent the team without over identifying with them. One solution is to have clearly defined roles for each member. In addition you need to:

▶ set and maintain group standards;
▶ involve staff where possible in objective setting;
▶ encourage new ideas, staff training;
▶ keep staff well informed on child care and other issues;
▶ have clear procedures, for example – grievance, appraisal.

THE INDIVIDUAL

You must try to understand those working alongside you and make sure that you:

▶ give feedback so that staff feel a sense of personal achievement in their work with children;
▶ delegate responsibility to match capability;
▶ give adequate recognition for achievement;
▶ provide opportunities for staff to develop.

Theories of leadership

Studies of leadership examine why some leaders appear to be more effective than others. We shall discuss:

1 Path Goal Theory
2 Fiedler's Contingency Theory

PATH GOAL THEORY

Path Goal Theory, developed from the work of M. Evans (1969), looks at leadership effectiveness from a variety of situations. As it is a very complex theory, only the basic framework will be considered here. Path Goal Theory depends upon the idea that leaders should set achievable goals and make it clear to staff how to attain these goals (the path). The application of Path Goal Theory in practice increases levels of job satisfaction, motivation and ought to lead to a positive outcome and reward. Staff benefit as they feel they have achieved something. Path Goal Theory encompasses four styles of leadership:

- Directive
- Supportive
- Participative
- Achievement oriented.

The style of leadership you use depends on the situation. You will be able to see the possible links between leadership style and the three elements of the process of leadership: task, team and individual.

1 **Directive leadership** This style involves giving clear guidelines to staff. Staff are aware of what is expected of them as they are told who does what, how, when, where and with whom. This is a strong style of leadership with clear rules and procedures that must be followed. This style is most effective, for example, with students on placement and new staff. They can leave the problems to you, the leader. It is also effective when the task is ambiguous, because you can clarify what needs to be done.

2 **Supportive leadership** This style includes giving consideration and showing concern for others. The leader is friendly and relaxed and tries to make work an enjoyable experience. It is an effective form of leadership when staff are competent and highly motivated. Studies show that if the task to be completed is stressful or boring this supportive style of leadership can enhance job satisfaction for the team.

3 **Participative leadership** This style is characterised by shared decision-making. Staff participation at all levels is good. This form of leadership is seen very often in the management of playgroups. Participative, like supportive, leadership is most effective when the team is highly motivated.

4 **Achievement oriented leadership** This style places emphasis on achievement and excellence. Challenging goals are set and there is an expectation that staff will take personal responsibility for fulfilling them. Staff with an intense need for achievement will respond well to this style.

FIEDLER'S CONTINGENCY THEORY

This theory is based on the idea that a leader's effectiveness depends on interaction between the leader's approach and the situation in which they are leading.

Fiedler (1967) suggested that there are basically two types of leader, the task person and the people person (see page 26).

According to Fiedler's Theory, leaders who are people-oriented are most effective when situations are moderately favourable, but are less effective in highly favourable situations. Leaders who are task-oriented do better in situations which are highly favourable or are highly unfavourable.

▶ The people person leader in a **moderately favourable situation:** the people person leader functions best when difficulties are caused by both **task** and **people**. The people person will recognise the task reasons but will give the people the benefit of the doubt and try to solve the problem whilst keeping the people happy.

EXAMPLE

The playgroup manager asks Xanthe if she could take on the role of First Aider and deputy manager for the setting as Megan is off ill. Xanthe feels pressurised as she now has more responsibilities than she can comfortably cope with. However, she appreciates the dilemma of the playgroup manager and grudgingly accepts. The play group manager recognises that Xanthe is stressed as there are too many tasks and too few (human) resources. She offers Xanthe more money for the added responsibility and promises to advertise the post as soon as Megan's diagnosis is confirmed.

▶ The people person leader in a **highly favourable situation**: in this situation the people are not the problem. Everyone is hard working and pleasant. Staff go along with anything that the people person leader says or suggests as they do not wish to cause difficulties or angst. It is in this situation that the leader can become a 'popular failure' as the staff do not outwardly object to anything. In turn there is no wish by the leader to upset the staff or disturb the status quo.

EXAMPLE

Mrs Billett the newly appointed manager from within the team had little cause to alter the running of the nursery. She was pleased that the staff had approved her appointment and promised to continue the work of her former boss. All the staff were pleased with this promise.

▶ The task person leader in a **highly favourable task situation**: the task demands immediate attention. There is no time for consultation and individuals irrespective of their rank, profession or seniority are told what to do. People are less important than the task because the end justifies the means.

EXAMPLE

In the middle of an inspection visit and while there is also a parent on an induction visit, an explosion takes place in the kitchen and a raging fire ensues. The carer manager immediately orders her four staff members simultaneously: 'Inspectors, parent and children leave what you are doing immediately and all follow Anna (she is handed the register) to the end of the garden, Cathy telephone the emergency services, Lauren close all the doors and windows, Beth check the toilets.'

▶ The task person leader in **a highly unfavourable task situation**: there is a problem and the cause is not obvious. As in the highly favourable situation the task demands immediate attention but in this situation there is no obvious solution. The task leader can say, 'I don't care what is causing this but this is what I am going to do and impose draconian methods'.

EXAMPLE

There is low morale in the nursery. There is talk of some staff not pulling their weight and others seeking favouritism. Staff absenteeism has noticeably increased since the nursery received the inspection visit date.

The task leader calls a staff meeting to raise concerns. She imposes strict timetables. She sets individual work plan deadlines, diaries a curriculum planning development day for the entire staff team and gives each member of staff an appointment date to meet with her.

A basic assumption of Fiedler's theory is that personality cannot be changed; therefore if you find yourself in the wrong kind of situation, you will not be an effective leader. What is needed, therefore, is to change the situation and not the leader! You cannot assume that you will always be successful as a leader just because you have all the prerequisite personal qualities. You must also take into account the situation in which you find yourself.

Leadership style and group performance

Although leadership styles have been given different descriptive names by various authorities, when examined closely they all fit into similar categories. R. Likert (1961) described 'job centred' versus 'staff centred' management, whereas F.E. Fiedler (1967) makes the distinction between 'permissive' and 'directive' modes of behaviour. Other words used to describe these concepts have included 'task oriented' (autocratic) and 'people centred' (democratic) styles.

Lewin, Lippett and White in their classic study (1939) give us three leadership styles which are applicable to child care:

1 **Autocratic** The carer manager chooses to dictate to staff without consulting them or listening to opinions.
2 **Democratic** The carer manager discusses options with staff and agrees on the best solution.
3 **Laissez-faire** Carer manager leaves staff to their own devices and dissociates themself from any responsibility or blame.

These styles are on a sliding scale from autocratic through democratic to laissez-faire (see below). This means that the more power the leader has the less power the staff member has and the more power the staff member has the less power the leader has.

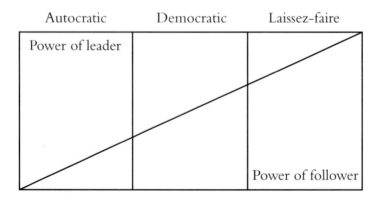

The 1939 study showed that under the **autocratic leader** there is generally more submission, deference and control when the leader is present. In the absence of the autocratic leader there is usually disruption and aggression. Problem solving leads to frustration and blame.

Under the **democratic leader** relationships are better. There is less aggression, more respect for each other and the leader is approachable.

There is calm and cooperation even in the absence of the leader and generally more is achieved.

Under the **laissez-faire leader** there is little or no interference or direction from the leader. The groups are chaotic, staff are aggressive to each other and very little work is done whether the leader is present or not.

It appears that the democratic leader achieves the best results through giving an explanation and encouraging participative decision making. Feldman and Arnold (1983) state that:

> *Individuals under democratic leadership were more satisfied, had higher morale, were more creative and had better relationships with their superiors.*

Leadership in practice

Effective leadership is a two-way process between leader and team. What we need to look at is **how** the leader gets the necessary power to control and influence staff.

SOURCES OF POWER

French and Raven (1959) from their analysis of organisational power identified five types of power that a leader may possess: reward, coercive, legitimate, expert and referent. The most effective leaders seem to have access to all five sources of power. The source of power comes from a combination of the leader's personality and their position in the organisation.

1 **Reward power** Your power will increase as a leader if you take time to supervise your staff and give appropriate praise and recognition for good child care practice. If you can develop your staff's potential or keep them up to date with child care issues, you will add to your reward power.
2 **Coercive power** The opposite of reward power, meaning that you, as leader could use your power to punish staff, for example, through threat of dismissal if they fail to uphold the management line.
3 **Legitimate power** The power conferred upon you by your position within the setting. For example, you may have access to a confidential file on a child but this access is denied to your staff.
4 **Expert power** Your personal abilities and expertise. Staff are able to see you as expert in a wide range of tasks, e.g., comforting a distraught child, dealing with an angry parent, delivering effective long-term plans.
5 **Referent power** Occurs when staff rely upon you as their leader or model themselves on you. The more they do this, the more referent power we can say you have as leader.

There is no guarantee that if you have access to all five sources of power you will be an effective leader. Effective leadership depends on how you decide to use your power, i.e. what you influence your staff to do.

Deciding how to lead

It is important to look at what factors or forces a leader should consider in deciding how to lead. Three are of particular importance:

- ▶ Forces in the leader   – deciding what is your leadership style.
- ▶ Forces in the staff   – understanding what motivates staff.
- ▶ Forces in the situation – the nature of the setting, number of children, resources.

The strength of each of the above will vary from situation to situation but as a leader if you are sensitive to them you can better assess the situation and determine which style of leadership is most appropriate. In Chapter 7 we will consider motivation and the needs of staff.

Controlling

As a carer manager you will have the ultimate control over everything that goes on in the setting. This does not imply autocracy. Rather it involves knowledge gained through constant appraisal, observation, assessment and evaluation of:

- ▶ your basic provision;
- ▶ children's progress;
- ▶ learning programme;
- ▶ staff effectiveness;
- ▶ resources.

The inter-relationship of planning, leading and control

Planning	Leading	Control
DIRECTION	Gives a sense of direction and attention to educational goals	Guides activities towards Desirable Outcomes for Children's Learning
STAFF	Motivates carers	Rewards carers for effective practice
POLICY	Anticipates problems	Implement procedures
RESOURCES	Assigns the resources to the six areas	The effective use of the resources

Of the entire management process, the control function is one of the major determining factors. In child care, control as a management function ought to guarantee that organisational aims inform planned activities. **Planning**, **leading** and **controlling**, as elements of the management process, are interrelated to the extent where good planning and leading includes control systems. Planning, leading and controlling must be integrated for effective performance. The preceeding gives an indication of the areas of inter-relationship.

These inter-relationships show how important it is for the elements of the management process to be integrated if effective performance is to occur. Control can give a clear indication as to how effectively the other management functions of planning, leading and organising are working.

Industry uses three types of control: **input controls**, **process controls** and **output controls**. Though not a product industry, some aspects of this model can be applied to child care in each of the areas below:

▶ children's progress;
▶ effectiveness of learning programme;
▶ staff performance;
▶ use of resources.

Children's progress

Children come to your setting at various ages and stages of development; applying the industrial model of control we can begin to look at the progress of the individual child.

Measuring the progress of the child: when to use input, process and exit controls

Child Assessment	Individual Programme	Type of Control
On entry	When they first start at your setting	Input controls
On programme	Duration of time spent with you	Process controls
On exit	Progression on to primary school	Exit controls

INPUT CONTROLS

This refers to the entry criteria in terms of your setting requirements. As carer manager you can specify whether for example, your provision is for 2–5 year olds or from three-month-old babies to two year olds.

PROCESS CONTROLS

This refers to monitoring and evaluating the standards of the child. For example, in the area of language and literacy, not only are you providing a print-rich environment but you are also monitoring:

▶ the child's progress;
▶ the child's ideas;
▶ the child's understanding of a story;
▶ child's ability to relate some aspect of the story.

Through observation on a daily, weekly, monthly, three monthly and annual basis you can assess how the child is progressing.

EXIT CONTROLS

In educational circles, the above progress is referred to as 'value added'. How far you have got with preparing this child for their next stage? In the case of a child with special needs, where progress is less evident, you need to monitor more closely to assess what achievement they have made during the time spent with you.

Effectiveness of learning programme

With specific learning outcomes for each child and through individual assessment you will be able to track the child's progress and assess the effectiveness of your learning programme. If, for example, all the children have made significant progress in working toward the 'Desirable Outcomes for Children's Learning', then you will be evaluating the level of your expertise and that of your carers as well as monitoring and evaluating your strategic plan (see page 34).

Each individual's needs are unique as are each group's: what was effective last year will not necessarily satisfy the current child or group. You will have an ongoing system for evaluating children's progress and current interests. This gives you control over the curriculum that you present in all areas of learning. You will be evaluating what the children have learned from your provision on a day to day basis through filling in your weekly and daily planning sheets. You can gain control over how you and your staff present your curriculum through evaluating what worked and its effectiveness as well as what went wrong.

Staff performance

This includes monitoring standards of the carer: their task level and their interactive skills with children and adults. Through an ongoing staff appraisal programme, you will be able to draw up action plans with carers and present relevant staff development training. As a carer manager you will be responsible for the effective deployment of your staff. An important aspect of this is the allocation and use of time for the various tasks that must be accomplished.

Use of resources

You will have to control your material, manpower, money and minutes.

MATERIAL

From time to time it will be necessary to carry out a curriculum audit to ensure that your basic resources are being used in a balanced way. For example, in the area of physical development, you might assess whether children have access to a variety of small and large apparatus. An activity grid can be useful to assess which areas of your provision are being under-used.

MANPOWER

You will be able to recruit and select staff on the basis of your needs. You will need to evaluate and appraise their effectiveness and with them develop their particular skills and interests (see page 138).

MONEY

If you are to ensure that you achieve your strategic goals, then it is imperative that you have a thorough understanding of your expenditure and revenue over a period of time. You must budget. A budget is an important managerial tool as it informs each function of the management process namely: planning, organising, leading and controlling.

- ▶ **Planning** A budget will help you develop realistic goals and basic plans and policies linked with these goals.
- ▶ **Organising** Through budgeting, you will be able to coordinate the activities of your team, clarify and assign areas of responsibilities.
- ▶ **Leading** Budgets help you to realise your strategic goal through the implementation of your organisational plans. The leading function is a key part of this process.
- ▶ **Controlling** Budgets will compel you to use your human and material resources efficiently, value them and establish a means for periodic analysis or appraisal.

MINUTES

Peter Drucker's definition of effectiveness (1954) is doing the right job, knowing what to do and when to do it, investing your time for the greatest return. Other management consultants believe that Drucker should have included efficiency: doing the right job in the right way. The combination of effectiveness and efficiency is the key to the process of time management. As a carer manager, your productive use of time will be constrained by:

▶ the size of the provision;
▶ material resources;
▶ number of staff;
▶ number of children;
▶ the age and stage of their development;
▶ the duration of the session.

What are you making time for? How well does your present use of time or that of your staff fit in with your strategic plan?

ACTIVITIES

After reading this chapter you may like to complete some of the following activities.

1. How can the planning process be coordinated and made more effective?

You might like to consider the following issues in relation to this question.

▶ Strategic objectives must be clearly defined.
▶ Targets must be set.
▶ Think of change when planning for the long term, e.g. in technology, the environment.

2. What is your leadership style?

Think of some of the people with whom you have dealt in groups in the past, either at work or in social situations. Recall the person with whom you found it the most difficult to work.

Describe this person on the scales below. You should work quickly. The whole scale should take you less than two minutes. Circle the number that you feel best represents the individual concerned.

Scale to assess leadership style

Pleasant	8	7	6	5	4	3	2	1	Unpleasant
Friendly	8	7	6	5	4	3	2	1	Unfriendly
Rejecting	1	2	3	4	5	6	7	8	Accepting
Tense	1	2	3	4	5	6	7	8	Relaxed
Distant	1	2	3	4	5	6	7	8	Close
Cold	1	2	3	4	5	6	7	8	Warm
Supportive	8	7	6	5	4	3	2	1	Hostile
Boring	1	2	3	4	5	6	7	8	Interesting
Quarrelsome	1	2	3	4	5	6	7	8	Harmonious
Gloomy	1	2	3	4	5	6	7	8	Cheerful
Open	8	7	6	5	4	3	2	1	Guarded
Backbiting	1	2	3	4	5	6	7	8	Loyal
Untrustworthy	1	2	3	4	5	6	7	8	Trustworthy
Considerate	8	7	6	5	4	3	2	1	Inconsiderate
Nasty	1	2	3	4	5	6	7	8	Nice
Agreeable	8	7	6	5	4	3	2	1	Disagreeable
Insincere	1	2	3	4	5	6	7	8	Sincere
Unkind	8	7	6	5	4	3	2	1	Kind

Source: Adapted by Gibson et al., 1985 from Fielder and Chemers, 1984

▶ To obtain your score, add up the numbers you have circled.
▶ If you scored 57 or lower you tend to be task-oriented.
▶ If you have scored 64 or higher you tend to be people-oriented
▶ A score between 58 and 63 would suggest that there is a 'mix' of the two approaches in your leadership style.

3. HOW EFFECTIVE AND EFFICIENT IS YOUR TIME MANAGEMENT?

▶ List the main areas of your responsibility into seven components.
▶ Choose three as core components.
▶ Evaluate the time you devote to your core components.
▶ Look at each of the following task categories – working with children, phone calls, meeting parents, paperwork. What percentage of these relate to your major or core components? Is a high percentage of your time focused on non-essentials?

References

Drucker, P. (1954) *The Practice of Management.* New York: Harper.
Early Years Development Partnerships and Plans (1988). Sudbury, DfEE Publications Centre.
Evans, M. (1969) *Path Goal Theory.* New York: Random House.

Feldman, D. C. and Arnold, H. J. (1983) *Managing Individual and Group Behaviour in Organisations*. New York: McGraw-Hill.

French, J. R. P. and Raven, B. (1959) in Hayward, S. (1996) *Applying Psychology to Organisations*. London: Hodder & Stoughton.

Fielder, F. E. (1967) *A Theory of Leadership Effectiveness*. New York: McGraw-Hill.

Katzenbach, J. and Smith, D. in Montebello, A. R. (1994) *Work Teams that Work*. New York: PHD Best Sellers Publishing.

Lewin, K., Lippitt, R. and White, R. K. (1939) in Hayward, S. (1996) *Applying Psychology to Organisations*. London: Hodder & Stoughton.

Likert, R. (1961) *New Patterns of Management*. New York: McGraw-Hill.

Further reading

Handy, C. (1996) *Understanding Organisations*. London: Penguin.

Herzberg, F. (1966) *Work and the Nature of Man*. New York: World Publishing Co.

3

Managing Children's Needs

A professional approach to any task assumes a certain body of knowledge. In child care an integral part of sound management is understanding child development as this gives us an insight into the needs of children. All children have needs that must be met. This chapter concentrates on **cognitive**, **social** and **emotional** development in children. Case studies help to illustrate the management implications and provide the child carer and carer manager with an overview. There are core ideas in child care. All those involved in child care, regardless of their titles or roles, need to be aware of these: **learning begins at birth** and **all children have individual needs**.

The need for child care management?

Give me the child and I will show you the man

(J.-J. Rousseau)

Historical attitudes to children's needs

During the nineteenth century children were considered unruly, needing very strict discipline. By the early twentieth century, behaviourists like John Watson believed that children were like blank slates ready to receive patterns of acceptable behaviour. Watson wrote:

> *There is a sensible way of treating children. Treat them as though they were young adults. Dress them, bathe them with care and circumspection. Let your behaviour always be objective and kindly firm. Never hug and kiss them, never let them sit on your lap. If you must, kiss them on the forehead when they say goodnight. Shake hands with them once in the morning. Give them a pat on the head if they have made an extraordinarily good job of a difficult task. Try it out, and in a week's time you will find how easy it is to be perfectly objective with your child and at the same time kindly. You will be utterly ashamed of the mawkish, sentimental way you have been handling it.*

T. B. Watson (1972) The Psychological Care of the Infant. New York: Ayer Co.

Such strict training of children's habits changed in the 1930s and 1940s in response to the writings of Sigmund Freud and Arnold Gesell (1946). Freud influenced psychologists to urge parents to relax and allow their children to develop without frustration and repression of their impulses. The parents became essential in guiding the emotional and intellectual development of the child.

To avoid conflicts and neuroses, parents were advised to be lenient and understanding with their children. Gesell's studies of healthy, upper middle-class children led him to conclude that the pattern for healthy growth was **already** in the child and that growth would occur naturally if left alone.

Both Freud and Gesell stressed that the child's need to develop naturally had to be understood and met. Recent research, on the other hand, has shown that children need clear boundaries and guidance in channelling their natural impulses. Excessive parental permissiveness can create an unhappy child.

Identifying children's needs

Advances in the field of child development have altered our understanding of the child and the role of the child carer. There is now a range of models of child development.

1 Piaget's Theory of Cognitive Development
2 Bowlby's Theory of Attachment
3 Maslow's Pyramid of Human Needs
4 Kellmer Pringle's Primary and Secondary Needs

Each of the above models focuses on a different aspect of child development. Piaget emphasises intellectual development, Bowlby, social development and Maslow and Pringle, emotional development. In order to manage children's care and education effectively the carer must have a thorough understanding of how children develop in the above areas.

Piaget's Theory of Cognitive Development

Cognitive or intellectual development is the development of children's ability to think and to make sense of their environment through interacting with experiences and objects. It covers the changes in perception, memory, thinking, reasoning, concept-formation and problem-solving which occur as the child matures.

Jean Piaget (1896–1980), a Swiss biologist and psychologist, was interested in the evolution of children's thinking. He was fascinated by the difference between adults' logic and children's thinking. Piaget spent 50 years observing children, his own amongst them, in great detail. His Theory of Cognitive Development, though open to criticism, is a useful model for understanding how children think. Piaget's theory is relevant to child care management.

Piaget uses technical terms from his study of logic and biology to define his thoughts on the subject of child development. It is useful to define his terms before taking account of his theory of development. He identified four steps in the thinking process: **schema**, **assimilation**, **accommodation** and **adaptation**.

1 **Schema** (plural: schemata or schemas) is a basic element of Piaget's theory. It includes the memories, data and ideas that a child might have about an object or an experience, either genetically or from their surroundings.
2 **Assimilation** is the taking in of new information about experiences and perceptions and trying to fit it into existing schemas, templates or models.
3 **Accommodation** is understanding and processing information learnt from new experiences and modifying the existing schemas so that the new information fits.
4 **Adaptation** is the application of the modified model or schema to the next learning situation.

EXAMPLE

A four-month-old baby, who has always been breast fed, has taken in information through its experiences of feeding and organised this information into a **schema** for feeding which involves the breast. This is the process of **assimilation**.

If the baby is presented with a bottle containing the mother's milk, the baby will need much encouragement to accept the teat because the teat is a mismatch with their schema of feeding. The baby has to modify their schema of feeding to include the teat and modify their behaviour to fit the new conditions in order to feed from the bottle. This process of changing schemata Piaget terms **accommodation**.

When presented with orange juice in the same bottle the baby will not need encouragement to accept the teat because the teat has become part of the baby's schema of feeding. This application of the modified schema to a different food is **adaptation**.

In the above example, a state of disequilibrium arises when the baby experiences a mismatch between the teat and their schema of feeding. Through restructuring their schema of feeding to include the teat, a state of equilibrium is restored and the baby can feed. This is the process of **equilibration**, i.e. the balance between assimilation and accommodation.

The table below sets out the four stages of Piaget's Theory of Cognitive Development. He believed that all children pass through all stages in the same order but not at the same rate.

Piaget's stages of Cognitive Development

Age	Stage	Characteristics	Major Acquisition
0–2	Sensori-motor	Infant uses senses and motor abilities to understand the world. This period begins with reflexes and ends with complex coordinations of sensori-motor skills.	The infant learns that an object still exists when it is out of sight and begins to remember ideas and experiences.
2–6	pre-operational	The child uses symbolic thinking including language to understand the world. Most thinking is egocentric: the child only understands the world from its own perspective.	The imagination flourishes. Children gradually begin to de-centre or become less egocentric and to understand other points of view.
7–11	Concrete operational	The child understands and applies logical operations or principles to help interpret specific experiences or perceptions.	By applying logical thought and manipulative abilities children learn to understand the basic ideas of conservation, number classification and many other specific or concrete ideas.
12+	Formal operational	The adolescent or adult is able to think about abstractions and hypothetical concepts.	The idea that there are many answers to every question and many questions about every answer evolves.

Recent research has shown that stages can overlap chronologically and it is now thought that children learn in **sequences** rather than in stages.

In other words, children's learning in every area follows the same order and the same rules. Before you can help each individual child move on, you need to recognise where the child is in the learning sequence. This will ensure that the activities and experiences that you offer are appropriate to the individual child, rather than to the developmental expectations for that child's age and stage.

EXAMPLE

If you have a three and a half year old with delayed language you can provide opportunities for the child to hear language through simple, repeated commands and instructions and words for key actions. The use of picture story books, tapes, songs, rhymes adds further dimensions to language. Playing alongside the child, talking as you do so, can also help. Through activities such as block play the child will learn to count.

Piaget believed that children actively try to make sense of their environment and this is what motivates much of their behaviour. His theory looked at the way children learn through developing the ability to organise their everyday experiences. This they do through their play.

As a carer manager, it is important to realise that Piaget sees the learning process as the child acting on and adapting to their environment rather than experiencing it passively. This active engagement with the environment is essential in the process of cognitive development.

When planning the learning environment for the child, it is important to bear in mind the following criteria:

▶ You must know what the child has already learnt (i.e. their schemas) in order to advance the child's learning.
▶ Activities and experiences provided should be stimulating and appropriate to the individual child's age and stage of development for the assimilation of new ideas.
▶ The environment must make demands on the child, if new learning is to take place.
▶ The child needs time to become familiar with new learning through practice, investigation, experiment and play; if denied this time, the child cannot accommodate effectively and will be confused.

Much of early years provision is influenced by Piaget's Theory of Cognitive Development because it provides important guiding principles for those working with children.

Carers should have underpinning knowledge of Piaget's Theory of Cognitive Development and a thorough understanding of its application to the child's environment. Carers must be trained to carry out and record child observations and assessments.

These assessments will show the stage of development for each child and what skills each child has acquired. The informed carer can anticipate what skills each child will be ready to acquire next. As the child nears the end of one stage, the carers should prepare him to achieve the skills of the next stage. Materials and graded resources should be selected to help the child achieve mastery of the tasks of their current and potential developmental stage.

Knowledge of Piaget's theory will help you, as carer manager or child carer to identify each child's stage in the learning process. What you can reasonably expect from one child may be unrealistic for another. The learning process involves the child acting on and adapting to the environment. You have to manage the child's environment by making it appropriate to their stage of development. The environment should be stimulating and provide challenging experiences. 'Something new every day' is a good objective.

Bowlby's Theory of Attachment

Bowlby's Theory of Attachment will give you an insight into the formation of person–person bonds. It will show you as a child carer or carer manager that the bond you form with each child will influence their emotional, social and intellectual development.

John Bowlby (1907–90), a British psychiatrist, worked in the 1940s with mentally disturbed adolescents. In his research on their emotional development, Bowlby hypothesised that personality problems were the result of a disrupted or deprived maternal bond at a critical period in infancy. His later Attachment Theories provided the impetus for the study of social relationships in infancy. Bowlby looked at how and why infants form attachments and stated that these bonds in infancy:

> *were as important for mental health as vitamins and proteins for physical health.*
> (Maternal Care and Mental Health, 1951)

He was convinced that infants have a biological need to form an attachment and that the mother (or mother substitute) played an important role in this development. Bowlby's research focused on **attachment**, **separation**, **loss** and **grief** in childhood.

Central to his theory are the following ideas.

▶ The first five years of a child's live are most important in their emotional, social and intellectual development.
▶ Pivotal to this development is a child's relationship with their parent.
▶ Loss of or separation from a mother-figure (maternal deprivation) is a major cause of psychological trauma.
▶ This psychological trauma in childhood has far-reaching effects on character.

Bowlby believed that problems such as depression, delinquency and affectionless psychopathic behaviour resulted from maternal deprivation in childhood. Children need warm, loving relationships with their mother and other carers. This is why the key worker approach is very valuable in the care setting. In the key worker system, each carer is assigned a small number of children for whom they have sole responsibility.

EXAMPLE

In a care setting the key worker provides the link with home. Before the child enters the care setting, the key worker visits the family home, meets the parents and the child, and completes an initial assessment of the child in conjunction with the parents. This will enable the key worker to prepare for the child's individual needs prior to entry. The key worker will enquire about the child's interests and the need for a comfort object.

The key worker will also prepare the other children for the new child's admission. When the child first visits the setting, they will feel less intimidated because of the presence of the key worker.

Many of Bowlby's findings have been challenged as not entirely correct; for example, children do not necessarily become delinquents if the attachment bond is broken. **Michael Rutter** (1981) makes the distinction between **disruption** of affection and the **privation** of affection where children do not have the opportunity to form bonds of affection. Rutter believes that:

▶ There is a difference between final disruption, when a parent dies, and the **distortion** brought about by separation or divorce, where the parent can still be present.

▶ The quality of a family relationship is more important than the actual separation of the parents.

▶ The quality of support during separation is more important than the separation itself.

▶ Children can form relations with many people at the same time.

▶ Children are very resilient when deprived and suffer more from under stimulation than from lack of social contact.

Children can form relations with many people at the same time

However, in childhood, when an attachment is broken there is **separation distress** and an urgent desire to find the lost person. Schaffer and Emerson (1964) from their research with 60 babies lend some support to Bowlby's theory. They found three phases in the attachment of infants:

1 The **indiscriminate attachment phase** 0–6 months The child shows no particular preference for those around, whether parents or strangers. However, from three months, infants begin to show who they feel safe with – a milder form of the fear of strangers reaction.

2 The **specific attachment phase** 7–12 months This phase marks the start of the first attachment as the child wants to be close to the main carer. As a result, the child develops separation anxiety, usually related to the main carer, and fear of strangers.

3 The **multiple attachment phase** 12–18 months This phase usually begins approximately one month after the first attachment phase. Schaffer and Emerson found that, at this phase, infants were capable of forming an

increasing number of attachments and that they appeared to use different adults for different things; for example children preferred fathers for play and mothers when afraid. Multiple attachments could be with several carers. This finding suggests that childminding can successfully be divided among several carers.

Alternative types of parenting, as in the kibbutzim for example, contradict Bowlby's belief that there is a hierarchy of attachments with the mother or main carer at the top. Research has found that children are capable of making several attachments of equal value. Infants are more likely to form attachments with carers who offer them love and attention, as attachment is an emotional bond. Children need a friendly, caring atmosphere in which they feel secure.

Applying Bowlby's theory to practice

Bowlby's ideas about bonding are important in the management of children. If children are to feel valued and secure they need to form affective and stable relationships with carers. Carers will be responsible for the care of the child at a critical stage in their emotional, social and intellectual development.

Bowlby asserted that a baby makes one central attachment to one main carer. We now know that children can form multiple attachments to several carers. The strength and success of a child's attachment appears to depend not solely on continued presence and stimulation as much as on the quality of the time spent together. The child is more likely to form attachments to a carer who plays, laughs, talks and responds attentively for two hours a day than one who cares for them physically all day but does not play with them. The quality in relationship is developed through physical contact, hugs, hand holding, stroking, playing, and through enjoying one another's company with smiles, laughter and conversation. Quality time, apart from providing emotional comfort (trust and security), is very important in stimulating the child's thinking processes and thus promotes learning.

▶ **Induction practices:** children suffer varying degrees of separation anxiety and distress. This can be minimised through home visits and a flexible induction programme to meet the needs of the individual child.
▶ **Key worker:** although children can form attachments to more than one adult child care is more effective if the family is assigned a key worker who visits the home prior to the child care placement. This establishes a bond that lessens the initial fear and anxiety that the child would experience on entering a new environment.
▶ **Work planning:** preparation for table top activities and theme work

must be carried out in advance of the child arriving at the setting. The carer must be busied with the child and not with preparing detailed materials.

Maslow's Pyramid of Human Needs

Most psychologists have developed models of human needs based on adult behaviour. Maslow's model is one that can be applied to the management of children. **Abraham Maslow**, a popular New York Professor who died in 1970, proposed a hierarchical order of human needs and drives which is usually represented in the form of a pyramid.

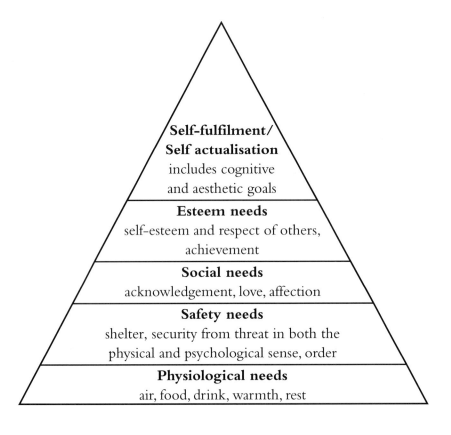

Self-fulfilment/
Self actualisation
includes cognitive
and aesthetic goals

Esteem needs
self-esteem and respect of others,
achievement

Social needs
acknowledgement, love, affection

Safety needs
shelter, security from threat in both the
physical and psychological sense, order

Physiological needs
air, food, drink, warmth, rest

The pyramid shows Maslow's theory of motivation in adults. As our primitive needs are met at each ascending level, the individual can progress to higher levels in the hierarchy. Once the physiological needs are met, the need for safety, security, order and predictability in life becomes important. Maslow assumes that we are driven to higher levels. The individual reaching self-actualisation will have fully utilised their potential.

Self-actualisation may be, for some people, the need to know and understand and for others the wish to live in a world of the aesthetic with beauty and harmony. As with other theories, the Maslovian Pyramid of Human Needs is only a metaphor. It is a generalisation that may not apply to all situations. Maslow assumes that if the basic needs are not satisfied there is no interest in the higher needs and if the lower needs are taken away we tumble down the pyramid.

Maslow's theory has relevance to child care. For example, a hungry or cold child will not be able to respond to your planned activities because their basic physiological needs have not been met. Similarly, children will not be able to learn if there is a threat to their security. You need to recognise and protect them from sexual, emotional and physical abuse (see Chapter 4). Once children feel safe in their environment they can venture outside themselves and address the higher need for acknowledgement and love through forming relationships. On the next level, self-esteem is essential to children's learning. The child's cognitive and aesthetic goals are part of self-actualisation in the Maslovian pyramid.

EXAMPLE

During their first week new children are often to be found attached to their key worker, comfort toy or looking through the window awaiting their mother's return. In a happy and caring atmosphere with kind responsive staff the child gradually begins to feel emotionally secure in the new environment. Once the child has been drawn into their new environment, they will be able to relax and take part in the learning experiences.

APPLYING MASLOW'S THEORY TO PRACTICE

The child's physiological and safety needs must be met in the setting. It is important to create an atmosphere where children feel respected and cared for. High learning achievement is related to high self-esteem. Given this support the child can work to the best of their ability within the curriculum you have devised.

Maslow's theory has no clear practical application but it is of value as a guide to ensure that all types of needs are considered. The various levels of need can overlap though the theory is described as an hierarchy. Therefore, Harry can be very popular with his peers (higher level needs) and yet be intimidated by his surroundings (lower level needs). The main asset of the theory is its intuitive appeal. Love and esteem needs follow safety needs. Observation and assessment of children is *how* the carer can use this theory to understand the needs of children and implement an individual play plan accordingly. Establishing the care and help needed to enable children to realise their potential is the most important practical aspect of Maslow's theory.

Kellmer Pringle's Primary and Secondary Needs

Kellmer Pringle (1920–83) identified children's needs as **Primary** and **Secondary**. If children are to survive, their primary needs for warmth, food and drink, shelter and clothing must be met. Kellmer Pringle defines secondary needs as interrelated and inter-dependent. This inter-relationship of needs has important implications for child care management. Kellmer Pringle's secondary needs in childhood are as follows:

▶ The need for love and security.
▶ The need for praise and recognition.
▶ The need for new experiences.
▶ The need for responsibility.

THE NEED FOR LOVE AND SECURITY

Children have an anxious journey to independence. The child instinctively wants to move away and become more independent, but separating from the parent figure may be difficult. Children deal with this anxiety in their own way. In their first year their need for security may be met by having a favourite toy, blanket or other beloved object which Winnicott (1974) called a **transitional object**. This object has certain qualities that remind the child of a person; the parent, or the main carer. The warmth, touch or smell of the object provides the child under stress with a sense of comfort and emotional security that is often needed at transitional moments such as preparation for bedtime or starting nursery. The transitional object can help the child pass gradually from dependence and attachment to independence. The intuitive carer will understand and respect this need in the child, which may last for many years.

> EXAMPLE
>
> Haruki's family has recently moved house. He started bringing his much loved and bedraggled comfort blanket to playgroup. This is interfering with Haruki's play at the clay table. Although his key worker, Nita, is sympathetic to Haruki's emotional need for comfort she decides to discuss the situation with Haruki's mother.
>
> Nita suggests that Haruki could bring a small pocket sized piece of the blanket to the playgroup to provide reassurance during this unsettling period. The larger blanket could be kept for bed time use and become part of the evening story routine. Haruki's mother agrees that this is a good idea.

Another aspect of the child's need for love and security is the need for routine and predictability. Carer managers and child carers must satisfy this need through, for example, the telling of a story at a particular time in a particular place. Children resist change at certain ages and meeting this need for routine helps the child feel acknowledged and independent, which leads to a feeling of self-esteem.

> EXAMPLE
>
> Jasmine had been attending nursery for two months. Every morning when she arrived she chose the same alphabet jigsaw. Her key worker, Abdul, decided that it was time to introduce Jasmine to more challenging jigsaws. The dialogue went as follows:
>
> 'Jasmine, look, we have a brand new jigsaw. Would you like to be the first to try it?'
>
> 'No, I want to play with the alphabet jigsaw.'
>
> Abdul then asked Jasmine: 'Could you please help me with this new number jigsaw and then I will help you to do the alphabet jigsaw?'
>
> Jasmine agreed and was delighted with her success. The following day she chose the number jigsaw first and proudly showed the rest of the children how to do it. Jasmine still favours the alphabet jigsaw but now has the confidence to do a wide range of jigsaws.

Pringle, like Bowlby, identifies the children's need to have a steady, durable and caring relationship with **empathetic** adults. The key worker system goes a long way towards answering these needs. Children need unconditional love, irrespective of who they are or how they behave. John Bowlby's studies of attachment stress how important children's needs for love and security are, especially in the first five years of life.

THE NEED FOR PRAISE AND RECOGNITION

Children need to be recognised and praised so that they will continue to seek knowledge about the world. Children need encouragement and incentive to achieve. Children feel like failures when they cannot live up to the unrealistic hopes of their parents and are less likely to try to repeat their efforts. The lower the expectation of the carer, the lower the level of effort and achievement of the child, sometimes called the **self-fulfilling prophecy**. Through interaction with others we gain knowledge of ourselves. Children build the opinions and reactions of others into their self-image, a process known as **introjection**.

EXAMPLE

It is Harry's third morning at playgroup. Harry doesn't like glue. He says, 'it's messy'. After much encouragement Harry sticks three boxes together. When Harry's mother collects him at the end of the morning, he runs to the door and shouts excitedly, 'Look Mum, I've made a boat'

The mother replies, 'Don't be silly, that doesn't look anything like a boat!' Harry bursts into tears.

The next day, Harry refuses to go near the sticking table, saying, 'I can't make boats'.

If you make children feel anxious because they have not succeeded they will shun activities likely to lead to failure. In the above example Harry is avoiding potential failure. It is your responsibility as carer manager to encourage all staff to praise children appropriately when they try hard or have achieved something new. This will motivate children to greater effort and even greater achievements, leading to the desire to achieve something for itself: **intrinsic motivation**.

THE NEED FOR NEW EXPERIENCES

Children learn from their experiences. As children pass through each stage of development they often return and work on a previous level in a new way. If new experiences are to be meaningful they should extend what children have already learned. These new experiences should present children with social, intellectual and physical challenges.

THE NEED FOR RESPONSIBILITY

Being responsible involves knowing what is to be done and how to do it. Responsibility comes when the child accepts a task and wants to complete it on their own. Children have different levels of understanding at different ages. You have to structure the environment to provide challenging tasks appropriate to each child's abilities. Children who can plan their own activities according to their different interest and ability levels get more involved in the learning process and so feel free to make decisions and assume responsibility. Nonetheless, cooperation rather than competition allows children more freedom to accept and exercise responsibility. It is your responsibility as manager to incorporate into your planning, activities that will involve group work.

APPLYING KELLMER PRINGLE'S THEORY TO PRACTICE

To apply Kellmer Pringle's theory to practice each carer manager must ask of their practice – how are the Primary and Secondary needs of children met within the setting?

▶ **Primary needs:** is the building suitably warm and safe? Are there spare clothes to cater for the child who is caught unawares by the weather or suffers an accident. If you provide meals, are they healthy nourishing foods, attractively presented? Are there adequate portions of the food?

▶ **Secondary needs:** is it a happy setting where the child knows that they are loved and cared for? Is the child given appropriate praise? 'A child may be praised, but may not be given real recognition' (Bruce, 1987). Is the child given early responsibility? Is the child presented with a stimulating environment that encourages experimentation and problem-solving?

The importance of play

Adults often undervalue play and give it second place to other aspects of family life but children learn from play. Children need to play. It was Susan Isaacs (1954) who claimed that, 'Play is the work of the child'.

Difficulties in play

As a carer manager or child carer continually observing children at play, you need to be able to recognise abnormal behaviour in play. A child acting out their anxieties through talking to an imaginary friend or smacking a doll may be tolerated as long as the child's playmates are not intimidated or shocked. No child should be allowed to make another child their scapegoat or victim in their play.

EXAMPLE

Erin had been behaving aggressively towards Sushma of late. Sushma, in tears, reported to her key worker that Erin had pulled her hair. The playgroup leader, who had observed the incident, gathered information from witnesses about the build-up to the hair-pulling. Satisfied that this was a case of bullying, the leader dealt with Erin whilst the key worker comforted Sushma.

The leader took Erin aside and calmly and firmly pointed out that, 'pulling hair hurts! That is why Sushma is crying'. The leader asked how Erin would have felt if her hair had been pulled. Erin got the message, avoiding eye contact. The leader, arm around Erin, affirmed that she was not cross with Erin, but with her behaviour.

The key worker suggested that Sushma and Erin work together on a large floor puzzle. She encouraged both girls and praised their co-operative behaviour.

Staff were concerned about Sushma because this was not the first incident when she had been the victim of Erin's bullying. They met to plan assertiveness strategies for Sushma, such as negotiating and taking turns, and tactics to improve her self-esteem, such as praising her achievements and pointing out her strengths.

Play can give the carer an indication of the child's emotional state. Although psychologists have stressed different aspects of play and its importance in child development most would agree that play is best viewed as part of the total development of the child.

Cognitive development theories of play

Piaget thought of play as a process in which the active child learns. Play enables children to work through what they already know (assimilation) and to understand new information about the environment (accommodation). Children learn best by acting on their environment and they do not distinguish between work and play before entry to statutory education.

Piaget also believed that different types of play corresponded to different stages of cognitive development:

1 **Sensori-motor stage** 0–2 years – mastery play or practice play involving the repetition of sensori-motor acts.
2 **Pre-operational stage** 2–6 years – symbolic or make believe play.
3 **Concrete operational stage** 7–11 years – games with rules.

Vygotsky (1978) stressed the role of adults in children's play. He believed that adults should get involved to extend play and to provide opportunities for learning.

Psychoanalytic theories of play

SIGMUND FREUD (1856–1939)

According to **Sigmund Freud** (1856–1939) we are emotional rather than rational beings. He believed that the child's level of emotional maturity is demonstrated in the way they play. The unobserved child at play is uninhibited (Free Child) and controls the environment to give them pleasure.

Playing can help the child's emotional development. If the child has suffered a painful experience, the resulting anxiety can cause an inner conflict which can hamper the child's development. To reduce this anxiety or to cope with it, the child falls back on what Freud called their **defence mechanisms**. The most obvious defence mechanism is **projection.** At play, the child may attempt to fulfil their deepest wishes through projection. For example, the child with a new sibling, longing to be an only child again, may continuously beat a doll.

Freud explained the structuring of the child's play as a striving for **homeostasis** (or balance). The child needs to keep the level of their nervous tension constant by repeating and thereby controlling a distressing event. Here, play is therapeutic, because the child can act out their inner anxieties and relieve their tensions. Indeed, play therapy used for highly disturbed or abused children has its roots in Freudian psychology.

EXAMPLE

Therapeutic play is used to allow the child to get in touch with and express their feelings. The therapist has to totally join in the play session and follow the dictates of the child. In *A Special Listen* Madge Bray

(1989) relates her account of a session with a little boy of three and a half years old. The little boy always seems to be smiling, but on closer examination the smile proves to be a facial contortion instead. In Bray's own words '. . . he had learned that if you smiled at the world, you increased the chances of the hand above you playfully tousling your head instead of clobbering you.'

On her third meeting they play together with a great big box containing large play equipment. His anger is suddenly triggered. He orders her, amidst a torrent of abuse, to climb into the large box. She has to obey his command to lie at the bottom of the box and cry. He screams abuse then opens the box and shouts at her to get out. He dons an ugly Halloween mask and demands that she be scared. Once shut in the box again, as punishment for admitting her fear, more screams of abuse follow. He throws bricks inside the box. Lying in the box, she says, 'I'm not going to let you hurt me'. In the midst of his fury he screams, 'If you don't shut up, I'll lock you in the shed again'.

It is only at this moment that Madge Bray really begins to understand what is actually occurring in his life. It is a clear example of how a disturbed child can use therapeutic play to express himself. It is the role of the therapist to enable the child to see the problem. In the above example, Madge Bray helps to make the strong unconscious feelings of anger and resentment conscious to the little boy.

D. W. WINNICOTT

Freud's theories were further developed by Winnicott in the 1970s. Winnicott (1974) regards the universal phenomenon of play as a thing in itself, a creative experience where the child is able to use their entire personality to discover the 'self'. In the therapeutic setting Winnicott sees play as a means of communication to understand the child's emotions. The infant is unable to use language effectively but is able to convey through play feelings such as anxiety, pain, anger and sorrow.

Freud's Psychoanalytic theory had already shown how these emotions could hinder emotional development. For Winnicott, the therapist must focus on how to get rid of these emotional blocks and foster the child's own growth processes. Play is very much a therapy, as it is through play that the healing of the 'self' can begin. If the therapy is to be effective, the child has to be allowed to play of their own accord, spontaneously.

In this state the child inhabits their own world. They withdraw mentally and focus on the play to the exclusion of all that is happening around them. The child uses whatever is in the immediate environment such as objects, toys or materials in the service of some design that comes from an inner world.

> 'Playing facilitates growth and therefore health; playing leads to group relationships; playing can be a form of communication in psychotherapy . . .' (Winnicott, 1974).

The importance of language

Children have a built-in need to communicate. Language gives children a channel for expressing their emotions and interacting with others. From studies of the child's earliest behaviour, psychologists now believe that there is a relationship between language development, the growth of intelligence and thinking, and emotional and social development. Children need language to develop their intellect and ideas. Language gives children a channel for expressing their emotions and interacting with others.

Linguists have identified universal patterns of language development that even deprived children and children with learning difficulties share. It is thought that children learn language partly as a result of innate processes (nature) and partly through environmental experiences (nurture).

Stages in language development

1 Pre-linguistic Stage 0–12 months

> ▶ The beginnings of language as seen in the communicative behaviour of babies – crying, babbling, cooing and smiling.

2 Linguistic Stage 12 months–5 years
   By 12 months:

▶ capable of imitating speech sounds;
▶ use 'jargon', inflected sounds which resemble conversation;
▶ use passive vocabulary – respond to simple commands, e.g. give me your cup;
▶ understand more than they can verbalise.

By 18 months:

▶ use an active vocabulary – they name familiar people and objects;
▶ use of echolalia (i.e. echoing what has just been said);
▶ may have 20 words.

By 2 years:

▶ use an active vocabulary containing around 50 words;
▶ use of telegraphic speech is pronounced, e.g. 'me go bath';
▶ participate in songs and rhymes.

By 3 years:

▶ use complete sentences;
▶ vocabulary develops rapidly;
▶ egocentric conversation during play shows they are beginning to use language to think;
▶ can express their ideas and hold simple conversations.

By 4 years:

▶ use an extensive vocabulary;
▶ use syntax (i.e. the rules for arranging words correctly in grammar and form).

BILINGUALISM

Children from a bilingual or a multi-lingual family may initially have difficulty with syntax if the grammatical structure of their home language is very different from English. With specialist help, they can quickly learn to become efficient communicators in English. They might be helped by home language teachers, bilingual assistants or English as a second language (ESL) staff. It is important that the development of the home language continues. This will give children the developed linguistic structure necessary to make good progress in reading and writing.

Difficulties in language

As a carer manager or child carer you have to recognise the individual linguistic needs of the child and make adequate provision for these needs to be met especially if the child is a non-English speaker, has a hearing impairment or has communication difficulties.

Hearing impairment is quite common in young children: one child in four may experience hearing loss before the age of seven. Some children have blocked ears associated with colds. Some suffer from frequent ear infections resulting in 'glue ear', which causes temporary hearing difficulties. Other children may have more permanent hearing impairment.

A child who watches your face intently as you speak or who does not respond when spoken to from behind may not be hearing you.

Parents will be able to supply any history of hearing loss and information on, for example, how to ensure that the child's hearing aid is working properly. Professionals, such as a peripatetic advisory teacher for children with hearing impairments, may visit to help find out what is wrong with the child's hearing, to give advice on how to make the best use of the child's residual hearing or to discuss what to include in the child's individual educational plan. The child may also have an educational support assistant who will visit to help with language acquisition. Other professionals may be involved with the child in speech therapy or a hearing clinic.

Carers may be advised to wear a radio aid microphone around the neck to enable the child to distinguish speech from background noise. If the child uses a sign language such as Makaton or British Sign Language, it is important for everyone in the setting to learn this too. By playing alongside the child with hearing difficulties in a small group, carers can encourage conversation and language development. When speaking to the child, ensure that your face is in the light and get down to his eye level so that he can read your lips. Place him near you when you are reading a story.

Communication difficulties in pre-school children may indicate a delay or a disorder. The delay will improve with time and may not require speech therapy. The disorder, on the other hand, will almost certainly need specific help. This can be sought through the health visitor, who may make a referral to a speech therapist or a child psychologist.

Hearing loss can cause language disorder because a child cannot reproduce speech sounds that he does not hear accurately. Many children with cerebral palsy and brain damage have speech disorders. Oral Apraxia/Dyspraxia (severe articulation disorders) make speech unintelligible. Some autistic children use language in such a strange way as to make normal communication impossible. Speech therapy may help.

Language delay can emerge in a child's receptive language (i.e. his understanding of language): he may have difficulty in listening or in responding to instructions. Language delay can also emerge in a child's expressive language (i.e. his use of spoken or written language): he may use a limited vocabulary, or may talk in single words at an age when sentences are the norm. The child may have difficulties with phonology (i.e. the way sounds are organised) and may substitute for sounds he can't make. His difficulty may be with grammar (i.e. rules governing correct word order) and may produce incorrect structures: 'I see she'.

Two distinctive clusters of specific speech abnormalities have been identified and named. The first is known as 'pragmatic speech difficulties'. Some children develop speech and language reasonably normally, but have difficulties in using language in a socially effective way. They have poor listening skills, fail to make eye contact, interrupt conversations, tend to limit topics of conversation to their obsessive interests. Often, they have very good comprehension of concrete words but cannot understand abstract words (e.g. kind, quiet).

The second cluster of specific speech abnormalities is known as 'disordered speech'. In this case, children learn to speak in a bizarre or 'disordered' way. They have difficulty in remembering vocabulary. They get words in the wrong order. They seem confused when spoken to and rely on watching others to know what to do.

EXAMPLE

Asok's home language is Punjabi. His parents and sister also speak English at home. Regardless of the language which initiates a conversation, Asok's replies are in English. Carers at the nursery school are concerned because Asok, aged 4, speaks mainly in 'gobbledygook' (muddled speech sounds) or echolalia (echoes heard speech) with the occasional bizarre interjection which takes everyone by surprise. He watches other children and copies what they do because verbal instructions confuse him. His unusual speech is causing problems for Asok socially: the other children exclude him from their imaginative play because he can't fit into their 'Let's pretend that' situations. The nursery school manager suggested that Asok be assessed by his health visitor who referred him for language therapy. The speech therapist administered language screening tests which showed low scores in the child's ability to understand linguistic concepts and sentence structure. There was a discrepancy between his acquisition of information and his ability to process this information when asked to follow instructions or when information was embedded in a sentence. It was concluded that he had difficulties with auditory processing (i.e. receptive language difficulties). Assessment of his interactional skills showed that he talked incessantly in order to avoid listening to others. This saved him having to process what others were saying. The speech therapist recommended speech and language therapy for Asok. There has been a marked improvement in his expressive language and interactional skills.

ACTIVITIES

After reading the chapter you may like to complete some of the following activities.

1. THINK OF TWO CHILDREN IN YOUR CARE: PERHAPS A HYPERACTIVE AND A PASSIVE CHILD.

▸ Which needs are uppermost for them at the moment?
▸ How can these needs be met?

2. HOW WOULD YOU MANAGE THE IMPORTANCE OF THE CHILD'S NEED TO PLAY?

▸ Do you give play priority in your child care management?

References

Bowlby, J. (1979) *The Making and Breaking of Affectionate Bonds*. London: Tavistock.

Bruce, T. (1987) *Early Childhood Education*. London: Hodder & Stoughton.

Bray, M. (1989) *Children's Hours – A Special Listen*. Shrewsbury: Nightingale Books.

Gessell, A. and Ilg, F. (1946) *The Child from Five to Ten*. New York: Harper and Row.

Isaacs, S. (1954) *The Educational Value of the Nursery School*. London: BAECE.

Kellmer Pringle, M. in Bruce, T. (1987) *Early Childhood Education*. London: Hodder & Stoughton.

Piaget, J. (1986) *Six Psychological Studies*. London: University of London Press.

Rutter, M. (1992) *Developing Minds*. Harmondsworth: Penguin Books.

Schaffer and Emerson (1964) in Davenport G. C. (1994) *An Introduction to Child Development*. London: Collins Educational.

Winnicott, D. W. (1974) *Playing and Reality*. Harmondsworth: Penguin.

Vygotsky, L. S. (1978) *Mind in Society*. Cambridge, Mass.: Harvard University Press.

Further reading

Bruce, T. (1996) *Helping Young Children To Play*. London: Hodder & Stoughton.

Bruce, T. (1991) *Time To Play*. London: Hodder & Stoughton

Winnicott, D. W. (1974) *Playing and Reality*. Harmondsworth: Penguin Books.

4

Managing the Environment

Most children are cared for by their mother in early life. However, some children may be cared for by someone other than their parent from birth until they enter the school system at the age of five. Although Local Education Authorities are not legally required to educate the child until the age of five, in practice 90 per cent of 4-year-olds are in primary school. Most children by the age of five years have experienced some form of non-parental child care. This chapter looks at the various forms of child care provision and the need to manage the environment.

Child care provision

The following descriptions give an idea of the variety of some of the child care provision available.

Childminder

A person who cares for children during the day in his or her own home for payment. Most childminders take in other children while still attending to the needs of their own families. All childminders are required by law to be registered with their local authority's Social Services department. The Nurseries and Childminders Act of 1948 established the regulation of childminders. This has been replaced by the Children Act 1989 which gives local authorities the opportunity to refuse to register individuals and organisations that do not meet certain criteria. Childminders are assessed on their fitness to look after children under the age of eight following a character check and an inspection and registration of their premises.

The National Childminding Association (NCMA) provides information and guidance to childminders. However, large numbers of childminders receive no support and although the majority still lack formal training many are taking advantage of National Vocational Qualification (NVQ) programmes. The service continues to increase, reflecting the needs of parents. In 1985 there were 144,908 child care places with childminders in the UK.

Today there are over 97,000 registered childminders providing 374,000 child care places. This expansion in provision has certainly helped working mothers. In addition, many local authorities sponsor the placement of 'priority' children in need with childminders as an alternative to day nurseries.

RESEARCH ON CHILDMINDING

The researchers Bryant, Harris and Newton studied some 66 minders in a comfortable part of Oxfordshire in the early 1970s. The minders were randomly chosen from the registered list. In total the minders were looking after 98 children. The main forms of data collection were interview, questionnaire and observation. Mothers were interviewed at home to allow the researchers to observe the children at home and at the minders. Unlike previous researchers, they found no shortage of toys or play materials and no cramped surroundings. The children spent three quarters of their day at the minders while the minders concerned themselves with their own family chores. The researchers, from their observations, were able to divide the children into three groups: lively, quiet and passive. Below are the results of their observations.

Observations of children in their home environment and at their childminder's home

Children	At home	At minders
29% lively group	Happy at home	Did find stimulation at minder
26% quiet group	Quiet at home	Engaged in solitary, repetitive play – children only waiting to go home
45% passive group	Quiet and good at home	Under-stimulated at minder

Source: Bryant, Harris and Newton, 1980

These researchers concluded that childminding seems to work well for those children who are happy at home, and who do find stimulation at the minders. However, those children who are not stimulated at home are unlikely to be stimulated by the minder.

Playgroups

These were initially set up as a response by women themselves to both the play requirements of their children and their own needs as mothers. Motherhood can be an isolating and lonely experience. The playgroup provides opportunities for carers to socialise and share child rearing experiences in a relaxed and informal atmosphere.

Church halls, libraries, club halls were, and still are, the normal venues for playgroups. There are over 410,600 playgroup places providing approximately 2 million children with part-time play opportunities each week. Playgroups are often run by management committees and they can also be privately owned and managed. As with childminders, all playgroups are subject to legislation under the Children Act 1989 and therefore have to be registered with the local authority.

Increasingly, more playgroup leaders are becoming qualified in response to the requirements of the Children Act 1989 and the need to prepare for inspection by the Office For Standards in Education (OFSTED).

Nursery schools

These are managed by private owners and by some Local Education Authorities. In all parts of the country, primary schools are extending their services to accommodate under fives in nursery classes in response to government funding for the education of 4-year-olds. Most Local Education Authority nursery school staff have qualified teacher status or are trained nursery nurses. There are also some volunteers. The government is proposing that all pre-school settings eligible for funding after September 1999, should have a qualified teacher involved. Increasingly, nursery classes have a curriculum that offers pre-school children planned activities to include wider experiences than they may have at home. Planned activities for children aged four years must provide opportunities that meet the 'Desirable Outcomes for Children's Learning' as set out by the government. This is further explored in Chapter 5.

Under Fives' Centres

Provision includes day nurseries and nursery classes. These are 5,500 in number and offer 161,000 places. These centres, maintained by local Social Services departments, no longer have as their sole function the provision of day care for children but cater in addition for the broader social needs of families.

Families and children are usually referred by social workers, health visitors or other professionals because the child or parent is experiencing health or social difficulties. Places are therefore allocated on the basis of individual family or child care needs. Apart from child care, each centre provides a range of services for parents and their children which could include workshops and support groups for parents, outreach work in the parent's own home, and a toy library.

Under Fives' Centres have four main aims:

1 To help the child grow fit and strong.
2 To help the child's social interaction through shared games.
3 To help the child's language and communication skills and intellectual development.
4 To help the child's emotional development through continuity and a sense of belonging.

Nannies

There is very little information available as regards the number of nannies in employment but it is estimated that there are around 100,000 nannies working in the UK. Nannies are primarily professionally trained, female, and employed solely for child care. Most nannies live in the employer's home.

It can be expensive to employ a nanny. As a way of reducing the cost, some parents are willing to share the services of a nanny with other parents locally. This arrangement has similarities to the way in which childminders work. However, nannies are exempt from local authority regulation and control unless they work for more than two families. As nannies are not registered, the standard of care cannot be monitored externally.

Private agencies that place nannies may give guidance over contracts of employment, the conditions of employment and resources that may be available. It is hoped that in the future, the employment of nannies will be regulated as is the employment of childminders at present.

Au pairs

These are mainly overseas students wanting to improve their English. They have no formal training in child care and their primary duty is to be in sole charge of children. They may be required to help around the house.

Carers in the above categories will normally be responsible for children in the following three periods of their life:

1 Infant – the first year
2 Toddler – 1–2 years
3 Pre-school child – 2–5 years

Managing the environment to meet the needs of the child

Parents should feed a child's curiosity by providing an enriched environment because the infant's powerful desire to learn will benefit from well-organised experience.

Bruner (1968)

Counting and sorting

In Piagetian terms, as discussed in Chapter 3, it is through acting on and adapting to their environment that a child learns. It is your responsibility as carer manager or child carer to provide a stimulating environment for each individual child in your care.

▶ The provider of child care, whether parent, child carer or carer manager, must bring to the child's environment a sound knowledge of child development. Central to physical development is the concept that human development follows a sequence:

▶ From head to toe: control of head precedes co-ordination of muscles in upper body followed by use of legs.

▶ From inner to outer: gross motor skills precede fine motor skills.
▶ From simple to complex: walking precedes hopping then skipping.
▶ From general to specific: general physical response precedes gestures then words (Bruce and Meggitt, 1997).

Babies learn about their environment through their senses. Jean Piaget called the period of childhood from 0–2 years the 'sensori-motor' stage. In this stage, the child learns through the senses and through movement. Piaget identified the following **six** stages of sensori-motor development which indicate the requirements for providing a stimulating environment:

Piaget's six stages of sensori-motor development

Stage	Age	Sensori-motor development
1	0–1 month	reflexes: sucking, grabbing, staring, listening.
2	1–4 months	first acquired adaptations: sucking a pacifier, grabbing a bottle
3	4–8 months	responding to people and objects
4	5–12 months	becoming more deliberate in responding to people and objects
5	12–18 months	experimentation and creativity: 'little scientist'
6	18–24 months	thinking before doing: experimental and creative

The different ages require different environmental stimuli for developing all five senses.

The importance of environment to the very young child

0–1 MONTH

Learning begins at birth. The neonate environment involves a close bond with her mother. The baby learns to recognise the smell, the feel, the taste and the sound of her mother. Her needs are entirely met by her environment. At this stage, babies show signs of social development through sustained eye contact and smiling. Mobiles, coloured objects and musical toys provide stimulation as do objects which can be sucked. It is important to cuddle, sing and talk to the baby and wait patiently for her response.

1–4 MONTHS

The baby will spit out the dummy when hungry and contentedly suck it when not hungry. She prefers faces to featureless circles and begins to identify the carer by voice and smell. The baby will hear noises and try to locate them. Her own body becomes a stimulus for play as she discovers her fingers and toes – sucking her thumb, kicking her legs or staring at her hands. Bath time and non-restrictive clothing facilitate learning experiences.

4–8 MONTHS

With the development of hand–eye coordination, she can reach for and grasp a desired object. Toys such as an activity centre stimulate this skill. Late in this period, most babies can sit unaided.

Babies of this age will repeat actions to get the same response: she will squeeze a toy which makes a noise and laugh at the result. She will appreciate rattles and squeezy toys. This is the age at which to introduce noisy toys and the first blocks. She will look for objects that disappear from sight. She enjoys nursery rhymes and close contact with other people. This is the age at which babble appears, so it is important to read and sing to her.

8–12 MONTHS

During this stage, she is beginning to use the pincer grasp (thumb and finger). She will examine objects before doing something with them. The areas of sensory development can be stimulated by offering her 'treasure baskets' – baskets full of interesting objects to explore through heuristic play. These were devised by Elinor Goldschmied. In heuristic play, babies are put in control of their own play with no adult interference or intervention. The baby sits on the floor, supported by cushions, and is presented with a basket filled with simple, everyday objects made of natural materials to mouth, suck, poke and explore. Objects might include: shiny paper, an orange, a lemon, chime bells on ropes, shells, large pebbles. The room is cleared of furniture and toys. Adults, quiet but alert, sit on chairs placed in a circle around the babies and observe with interest. They are available to help or comfort if necessary but they do not take the lead. Babies involved in heuristic play are given empty containers and junk material such as cardboard tubes, ribbon, elastic, large corks, table tennis balls. They fill and empty their containers as they explore (Cousins, 1996).

Heuristic play was invented by Elinor Goldschmied (1994) as a means of providing more stimulating play and opportunities to learn for sitting babies of six to nine months. Goldschmied herself says, there must be a commitment to what she calls the 'minute particulars'. There must be a commitment to the selection and management of the materials (at least 15 types of materials). Time management is important: heuristic play has to be presented regularly and staff need to be trained. Carers must have the right attitude to heuristic play because it only works if it is done properly.

Babies at this age want to imitate others dancing, fighting or reading. She will crawl towards objects and might even grab dangerous objects and react with rage if deprived of them. She associates objects with events – running water with a bath.

12–18 MONTHS

Toddlers vary actions to get different effects – hitting a drum with a pencil or hammer to get different sounds. At this stage, she is into everything and likes to take apart rather than build. She discovers how to pull objects to her.

18–24 MONTHS

At this age, she is usually mobile. Toddlers need activities which encourage practice of newly acquired large motor skills and which involve exploration of the environment. Brick trucks, prams and large wheeled cars are ideal. She needs to climb up and down stairs. Outings to the park and sessions on the local climbing frame are essential. There should be opportunities for sand and water play. Stacking and nesting toys and jigsaws develop fine manipulative skills as well as hand–eye coordination. She will combine actions to solve problems, like putting something down before opening a door. This period of development is characterised by the need for independence and a great deal of language development takes place. The carer can foster independence by encouraging her to feed herself using her own plate, cup and spoon. She will imitate the actions of others; for example the tantrums of older children. She will pretend that her doll eats or sleeps or that she herself is asleep. Conversation at this stage develops language acquisition, particularly if response, action songs and rhymes are encouraged.

Awareness of what actions to anticipate from the child at each age of development will enable the carer to react positively to the child and to make use of the stimulating environment to each child's best learning advantage. Language is a very important aspect of this environment.

Managing the pre-school environment for the two to three-year-old

Pre-school children spend most of their waking hours running, climbing, jumping, throwing, pushing, dressing or painting. At the age of two they are clumsy and fall down or bump into things. Many do not have the fine motor skills to pour a drink, cut food, tie shoe laces or do up their buttons, and may become frustrated as a result. It is the role of the carer manager to provide a safe, supervised outdoor area containing play equipment to encourage children's development of gross motor skills.

TWO-YEAR-OLDS

Two-year-olds can be very loving and tactile. On the other hand, this period is characterised by explosive emotions. Two-year-olds long to be independent but lack the judgement to realise that certain tasks are beyond their stage of development. For example, a two-year-old trying to kick a football will fail as they cannot yet stand on one leg. If children are thwarted, jealous or frustrated they may have tantrums. Fortunately, they can easily be distracted and the perceptive carer can avoid frustrating situations by using this characteristic.

EXAMPLE

Two-year-old Sun Yi is trying to kick a football and making herself cross over her failure. Her carer encourages the child to throw the ball instead of attempting to kick it. It flies through the air satisfyingly and bounces. Sun Yi's face breaks into smiles, and her carer praises her.

As the child approaches their third birthday they have a greater awareness of **self**. They know their name and position in the family. This is the stage when role play begins. The child is impulsive; they want everything that they see and want to do anything that occurs to them. The carer must:

▶ set clear and consistent boundaries for the child;
▶ help the child control their impulsive behaviour;
▶ take responsibility for the child's safety and social development.

Physically the child becomes more independent as they acquire skills such as coping with buckles, buttons and zips. They may also be independent in their toiletting.

THREE-YEAR-OLDS

The three-year-old has more developed gross and fine motor skills: can ride a tricycle, stand on one foot, control a pencil using their thumb and first two fingers, copy a circle and has good spatial awareness. It is the role of the carer manager to provide adequate equipment and resources that will promote the development of these gross and fine motor skills.

Emotionally, three-year-olds are less rebellious and more patient. The carer is still able to use distraction as a means of controlling their behaviour. The three-year-old seeks approval from adults. It is easier to reason or bargain with a child of this age as they can use language to negotiate. They need adult help to modify potentially difficult situations. They can de-centre, that is they can look at things from someone else's point of view. In their imaginative play on their own and with companions they can take turns and share. This is a period of irrational fears; common examples are fear of monsters and fear of the dark. They model themselves on adults and learn appropriate social behaviour.

EXAMPLE

Ayinda, aged three, suddenly developed an irrational fear of spiders. She screamed whenever play in the garden was suggested and refused to go outside. Her key worker, Yolanda, talked this over with Ayinda's mother, Ada. It appeared that Ada also feared spiders. When one was found in the bath, she had to ask her husband to deal with it. Yolanda suggested to Ada that her own reaction in the spider incident most certainly imprinted itself on her daughter. Both the key worker and the mother agreed to treat the child's fear seriously, to talk sympathetically with Ayinda and to encourage her to express her anxieties over and over again. Gradually over several weeks, Yolanda introduced Ayinda to Eric Carle's *The Very Busy Spider*, using its tactile properties to capture the child's interest. Slowly, gently and patiently she encouraged Ayinda to look at pictures of real spiders in books and magazines. In a craft session the children in the setting made smiley spiders from the cups of egg boxes. Although reluctant at first, Ayinda was intrigued and joined in. Eventually, she managed short trips into the garden, helped by Yolanda's calm reassurance, gradually spending increasing amounts of time out of doors.

Managing the environment for children with special educational needs

Under the 1993 Education Act, a child is defined as having **special educational needs** (SEN) if he has a learning difficulty which requires special educational provision to be made for him (see page 182). Under the Guidance to this Act, children in need and with disabilities should be integrated into provision attended by other children in the community in order to lead 'as normal a life as possible'.

The physical arrangements in the care setting may have to be altered to accommodate children with special needs. For example a ramp may be necessary to provide access to the premises and special toiletting facilities must be available. It is important to ensure that there are positive images of disabled adults and children in posters, photographs and books. Again, as carer manager or child carer you must be careful with language: do not allow the use of names of disabilities as insults. Words such as 'deaf' label children. Be positive and focus on strengths.

MANAGING CHILDREN WITH SPECIAL EDUCATIONAL NEEDS

If a child's difficulties are severe, they may have been diagnosed already. However, as many problems become apparent with the development of expressive language at the ages of three and four, you may be the first to identify a child's needs. If you suspect that a child has a difficulty, the following procedure could be implemented:

1 Check that the child has no sensory difficulties – can see, hear etc.
2 Identify the problem and get a baseline record of the child's current skill.
3 Work out why you think the problem has arisen (form a hypothesis).
4 Teach/practise/try any strategy to help overcome the child's problem.
5 Monitor the rate of progress – to see if your method is working.
6 Change your hypothesis as new information develops and go back to 4 and try again. (Thornton, 1997)

Types of SEN likely to be seen in an early years situation:

▶ general developmental delay;
▶ dyslexia;
▶ attention deficit disorder (ADD);
▶ attention deficit disorder with hyperactivity disorder (ADDHD);
▶ autism;
▶ Asperger's syndrome.

MANAGING CHILDREN WITH PHYSICAL DISABILITIES

Talk to the child's parents about the nature and extent of the child's specific problems and the educational implications. Learn more about the condition by reading. Draw up an individual educational plan (IEP) for the child. The following guideline might be used:

1 Identify the main concerns through discussions with parents and carers.
2 For each concern assess where the child is now and decide on the goal to aim for.
3 Work out the next target in the progression towards the goals for each of the main concerns.

4 Decide how you will know when the child has achieved this target.

5 State the target and what resources, time and approaches will be needed to reach it.

6 Set a time to review the progress and go back to step 1.

A standardised IEP form should be obtainable from the LEA, particularly for groups in Partnerships with LEAs.

Types of physical disability likely to be seen in an early years situation:

▶ Down's syndrome;
▶ hearing impairment (from slight hearing loss to profound deafness);
▶ visual impairment (from minor, remediable conditions to total blindness);
▶ wheelchair bound.

EXAMPLE

Managing a child with Asperger's syndrome

Children with Asperger's syndrome may do some or most of the following:

▶ avoid eye contact;
▶ want social contact but lack the necessary social skills (e.g. empathy, lack the ability to read body language);
▶ have obsessional interests (e.g. wheeled toys, trains);
▶ have areas of high skills (e.g. maths, memory);
▶ use pedantic, odd speech, perhaps related to their current obsession;
▶ resist change, need routine;
▶ have a clumsy, odd gait and poor posture.

Gareth, aged four, exhibited all of the above behavioural characteristics. His health visitor arranged for an educational psychologist to visit the setting in order to assess Gareth and give carers guidelines on how best to work with him. Gareth's obsessive interest is dinosaurs. It was suggested that carers use this obsession to capture his interest and thus improve his progression towards the 'Desirable Learning Outcomes'. They were advised to break tasks into small steps and prepare Gareth for any change in his routine. They attempted to develop his social skills through cooperative activities such as floor puzzles. Table, board, and card games, with dinosaur themes, encouraged interaction with other

---

children. A card game with dinosaurs' names and pictures was used to help Gareth recognise letters, phonemes and whole words. Further language interest was stimulated by a factual book about dinosaurs. Gareth has an area of high skill in mathematics. Model dinosaurs were used to improve his mathematical skills such as counting, sorting, sequencing, matching, etc. In general, carers avoided abstract ideas because he does not understand and switches off. In social situations such as circle games, when he could not cope, he was offered other activities.

Managing children's experiences through the senses

We learn about the world in which we live through our senses of sight, sound, smell, taste and touch.

LEARNING TO LOOK

When you visit an art gallery or museum you are enriched by what you see. As adults, we make time to look. Children need you as carer to provide them with such opportunities. All children need to be encouraged to use their eyes and think about what they see. They need to be given time from you for encouragement and guidance to look and discover things at their own pace. All too often, like the rabbit in Alice in Wonderland, adults are checking the time and moving children on with the all too familiar phrases 'hurry up' and 'come along'.

Children have a natural curiosity, a sense of the ridiculous, and they can focus their attention once their concentration has been captured. The visual impact of an unusual object, a rainbow, the budding of a leaf, or the melting of an ice cube helps to build up associations and memories which have a greater influence than you can imagine. Apart from the obvious pleasure that looking at interesting things can bring, it is very important for practical reasons. As a child carer or carer manager, you need to offer this aspect of their environment to the child through a variety of experiences. You need to help them make the best possible use of all their senses. This is especially important to a child with special needs.

If you personalise the environment it will be more meaningful for the child. You can involve the child in scrap books and interest tables. Unusual artefacts provide the opportunity to introduce cultural diversity. When you use children's own work to mount displays and mobiles it gives them a sense of belonging. All this encourages the child to look.

LEARNING TO LISTEN

Children's auditory receptors are underdeveloped and as a consequence they are unable to filter unnecessary sounds and thus be attentive. Psychologists have noted that constant noise is both over-stimulating and tiring for very young children (Penelope Leach, 1974). Some children can become intimidated by generalised noise. As a child carer or carer manager you need to teach the children to identify specific sounds from the variety of noises in their environment. Children enjoy using the environment to experiment with sounds: echoes, amplification, bangs. You can help the child to listen by using sounds to announce activities; for example, the tinkle of a bell for the mid-morning break. Using a tape recorder or activity tapes that encourage the child to participate are most helpful in developing listening skills. Special help is needed by children whose hearing is impaired.

Sound-making equipment can help children with some types of impaired hearing to develop the ability to track the direction of sound. For a child who wears a hearing aid, loud noises may be disturbing, as aids tend to amplify all sounds. Some children with very limited hearing benefit from a radio aid microphone, worn by a special carer. These radio mikes filter out background noise, making it easier for the child to concentrate on speech. The health visitor or speech therapist can advise here. A profoundly deaf child listens with his/her eyes and may lip read. Inclusion of such a child means that everybody in the setting must learn to sign even if only on a limited basis. Makaton is normally used with young children; British Sign Language may be an alternative. A specialist teacher or speech therapist could help you to learn a sign language: the Royal National Institute for the Deaf is a useful source of information. Another comprehensive resource is the Pre-school Playgroups Association (PPA, 1991) Information Sheet 9: *Helping the Hearing-Impaired Child*. This leaflet also contains many useful addresses.

LEARNING TO TOUCH

Small children are into everything. They explore with their hands. **Montessori** (1949) observed this and developed a learning methodology based on touch. She believed that children absorb information through their hands and especially through their fingertips. As a carer manager, how can you make the most of touch for the child? You need to provide a stimulating, tactile environment and activities which encourage children to use their hands. This is particularly important for visually impaired children. It is through tactile experiences that the child can come to appreciate the difference between hot and cold, rough and smooth, hard and soft, heavy and light. The child needs to use a variety of textures and materials and enjoy the sensations this stimulation brings.

LEARNING TO TASTE

Sigmund Freud wrote about the pleasure the young infant receives from feeding. Freud called this pleasure **oral gratification**. The infant, once fed, has a sense of well-being and contentment. As they develop, the child continues to use the mouth as a means of exploring their world. Children develop preferences for certain textures and tastes at a very young age and may be selective. Children can explore new tastes in food tasting sessions. You can introduce children to cultural diversity through taste. Children will enjoy festival foods such as Easter eggs, pumpkin pie, unleavened bread or Divali sweets.

LEARNING TO SMELL

Of all the senses, smell stimulates young children the least. Nevertheless, it is important for forming associations and memories. As child carer or carer manager, you will need to plan the environment with scents in mind and draw children's attention to smells. Children will learn to associate certain smells with blowing out candles on a birthday cake or making biscuits. Outdoors, children can be introduced to smells in the environment by planting and tending fragrant herbs and flowers in the garden. For children who are partially sighted this sense is particularly acute and imagination is required when introducing different smells into their world. On outings there will be different smells associated with the farm, the bakery and the flower shop.

Managing the physical environment

> *Children are active learners and if they are to develop the skills and competencies . . . they must be able to work and play in a safe and secure setting.*
>
> (Curtis, 1998)

As a child carer or carer manager, whether you are working in a church hall, community centre, school annexe or home you must ensure that the physical environment promotes children's learning and is safe.

The learning environment

Your task is to provide an environment where the child can flourish: emotionally, socially, physically, intellectually, spiritually and aesthetically. You should consider whether you have appropriate and sufficient space, materials and equipment organised in a way that enables each child to maximise their learning potential and become independent. Given the area and layout of your centre you must utilise the space provided wisely to allow adequate movement between activities and to accommodate the requirements of children with special needs. One way of arranging the setting is to take account of the fixed areas such as entrance, kitchen or garden and plan your activities taking these areas into consideration.

Quiet area

This is often located near the book corner. Children who are disturbed by noise need quiet places. Children enjoy making dens, playing alone or talking quietly together. It is important for children to be given opportunities to withdraw from peer play and the gaze of adults. Silva, Roy and Painter in the Oxford Pre-School Project (1980) showed that high quality, prolonged bouts of play occurred most frequently when children played privately together in small groups without adult intrusion.

The home corner

Much imaginative play and role play takes place in the home corner. This area should include movable furniture and props. These will include dressing-up clothes and a variety of tools and utensils all of which reflect a multi-cultural society. Toys in this area should promote images of all children. Although the home corner is another area of privacy, carers should intervene sympathetically to enable children to resolve conflicts and to extend their play.

Block corner

This area provides children with opportunities for problem solving and cooperative play. Blocks present children with concrete problems which encourage them to reflect and make judgements. This type of play often produces the most satisfying results when two or more children play together. Blocks encourage exploration of mathematical concepts such as spatial awareness, shape and quantity. Here the carer, in the role of facilitator, helps the child to test hypotheses that lead to solutions. There must be a range of sizes and shapes of blocks to cater for children of all abilities. Block play provides you, as the carer, with rich opportunities to observe and assess development in individual children.

Messy area

This is the area where creative activities such as painting, collage and junk modelling take place. Malleable materials such as clay may be offered in this area. The area must be well prepared in advance and provide opportunities for all children who wish to participate. There should be a wide variety of attractive materials and appropriate adhesives for children to select. For many children, it is the process of creation rather than the end product that is important. The role of the carer is to act as facilitator in this process rather than imposing pre-conceived ideas upon the child. It is essential to value the child's efforts.

SAND AND WATER

These areas can provide satisfaction for children's emotional needs. Play with both of these natural materials is therapeutic, enabling children to work through their anxieties and tensions. Tactile experiences of sand and water are also pleasurable. Play in these areas can become repetitive and boring. It is the role of the adult to plan provision that extends the learning of the child. These areas may be particularly helpful in developing the abilities of children with special needs. Play with sand and water can teach many mathematical and scientific concepts: volume, capacity, conservation, changes. Children experience tools and techniques when they use pumps, siphons, taps and water and sand wheels.

SCIENCE AND TECHNOLOGY AREA

In this area children gather information through the senses. They use this information to formulate conclusions and predict outcomes. They test their predictions through further experiments. Children use equipment such as magnets and mirrors. Items for children to take apart will enable them to explore how things work; such items could be old watches or radios. Sets of objects, for example a variety of brushes, can reinforce concepts such as size and function. Construction toys should provide opportunities for using gears, pulleys and levers. Children also learn about science through cookery. There should be opportunities for growing plants.

INTEREST TABLE

Children enjoy bringing treasured items from home for the interest table. These provide opportunities for discussion, exploring and experimenting and will enhance children's knowledge and understanding of the world.

COMPUTER AREA

Play with computers develops the child's cognitive skills. It improves concentration and encourages memory and recall. Keyboard skills involve hand–eye coordination which is essential to writing.

LITERACY CORNER

A well prepared learning environment must provide opportunities for speaking, listening to stories and nursery rhymes, reading and writing. A variety of reading material must be available including books with texts, picture books, reference books, books which children have made, magazines and junk mail. Books should present positive images of people of all cultures and abilities. Tape recorder and story tapes will encourage individual listening skills and promote concentration. Mark-making instruments, for example: pens, pencils, crayons, ink pads and stamps and various sizes of paper must be readily available to encourage emerging writing skills.

A variety of reading material must be available

MUSIC FACILITIES

Children need opportunities to explore sounds and make their own music. Instruments should be accessible to all children. Listening skills, sound discrimination and the ability to recognise and repeat rhythms are essential to the learning of language. Making music in a group encourages social skills such as taking turns and sharing. Music can help children understand the culture in which they live and give them a sense of belonging. Music can provide a link with other cultures. It is important to introduce the children to a variety of instruments which produce sounds in different ways. Tape recorders are useful as they enable children to listen to music and to record their own performances.

OUTDOOR ENVIRONMENT

Playing outdoors is a very important part of the learning process, providing children with a wide range of opportunities for active physical experiences. Outdoor equipment may need to be adapted for children with special needs. The variety of outdoor apparatus should include a climbing frame for exercising large muscles and developing climbing and swinging skills. There should be wheeled toys for pedalling and steering. Bean bags and balls help to improve hand–eye coordination. A tunnel will teach the skill of crawling through. Other large equipment might include a slide and a trampoline. Children practise further skills such as starting and stopping, running, balancing, hopping and skipping. These skills encourage self-confidence and self-esteem and give children power over their environment. In the garden children have opportunities to observe the natural world. They learn respect for living and growing things. They become aware of the passage of time through the changing seasons. They learn concepts of height, width, speed, distance and growth.

Managing the secure environment

Safety

All early years settings must comply with:

▶ The Children Act 1989
▶ The Health and Safety at Work Act 1974
▶ The Food Safety Regulations Act 1995.

Further information on these Acts is given in Chapter 10.

Accidents and emergencies

By law, as carer manager, you must ensure that there is one designated member of your staff responsible for first aid and the first aid box. This person must have a basic first aid qualification with specific reference to children. There must be at least one qualified first aider in the setting at all times. In an environment dedicated to children it is inevitable that some injuries will occur and it is vital that staff have an understanding of the correct procedures to follow. An up to date first aid book to refer to is most important.

All the children's registration cards must give the following details

▶ the name and phone number of the parent or home carer;
▶ an emergency contact;
▶ name of GP;
▶ names of drugs or medications the child may be on;
▶ any known allergies.

Childminders should also keep such registration cards.

All injuries, however slight, should be recorded in an accident book and should include:

▶ name;
▶ date;
▶ time;
▶ injury;
▶ how injury occurred;
▶ treatment given;
▶ witness.

> At these ages [children aged three and four] many children do not appear to have a concept of 'accident' or 'danger'. The research suggests that those who do have such concepts have usually had some personal experience, but may not generalise from this to accidents in other settings. Lacking an accident concept most children appeared also to have no concept of cause or prevention.
>
> (Source: Gill Coombs, *You can't watch them twenty-four hours a day.*
> The Child Accident Prevention Trust, 1991)

IN AN EMERGENCY
▶ Do not attempt to take the child in your car to hospital.
▶ If the child requires hospital admission **call an ambulance** – dial 999.
▶ Take all medical records with you.
▶ Notify parents.
▶ If parents are unavailable, emergency contact must be notified.

ACTIVITIES

After reading the chapter you may like to complete some of the following activities.

1. FOLLOWING THE EXAMPLE OF THE FIRST CATEGORY (AU PAIR), LIST THE ADVANTAGES AND DISADVANTAGES OF THE VARIOUS FORMS OF CHILD CARE BELOW.

Carer	Advantages	Disadvantages
Au Pair	Lives in	Not child care trained Should not be in sole charge
Nanny		
Playgroup		
Nursery (LEA)		

2. USING THE CHECKLIST BELOW SEE HOW MANY OF THE 21 ITEMS YOU HAVE AVAILABLE.

Checklist for providing a pre-school environment

1   Indoor area is in good condition

2   Rooms are large enough and uncluttered

3   Rooms are bright, airy and well lit

4   Furniture is comfortable and adequate

5   Quiet corners

6   Puzzles, small blocks and table-top games

7   An area for make-believe play

8   Box of dressing-up clothes

9   Home corner: pots, pans, food

10   Dolls, clothes, telephones

11   Area for art work with tabards, brushes, paints within reach

12   Small world toys, building blocks, animals, cars, people

13   Area for looking at books and reading stories

14   Carpeted area with floor cushions

15   A cassette player, story tapes

16   Technology: mechanical toys, robots, computer

17   Water and sand area

18   Place for carpentry

19   Pictures, displays of the children's work

20   Signs of science activities such as animals, scales, plants, magnets

21   Outdoor space with safe equipment

3. EXPLAIN HOW EFFECTIVELY YOUR PREMISES, MATERIALS AND EQUIPMENT ARE USED?

▶ Think about the layout of your indoor area.
▶ Can the room be rearranged to improve movement between activities?
▶ Is there a range of activities available?
▶ Do the children have access to materials?

4. PLAN ACTIVITIES TO TEACH CHILDREN HOW TO USE EACH OF THEIR SENSES.

▶ Make use of the indoor and outdoor environments.
▶ Can you develop children's senses through creative activities?

5. PREPARE A BOOKLET FOR PARENTS ON ATTENTION DEFICIT DISORDER (ADD).

▶ What are the signs and symptoms?
▶ What are the educational implications?
▶ What are the strategies for management?
▶ Provide a list of support networks.

Useful Addresses

Royal National Institute for the Blind (RNIB)
224 Great Portland Street
London W1N 6AA
Tel: 0171 388 1266

SCOPE
6 Market Road
London N7 9PW
Tel: 0171 619 7100

Royal National Institute for the Deaf (RNID)
105 Gower Street
London WC1E 6AH
Tel: 0171 387 8033

Pre-school Learning Alliance
61–63 Kings Cross Road
London WC1X 9LL
Tel: 0171 833 0991

References

Bruce, T. and Meggitt, C. (1997) *Child Care and Education*. London: Hodder & Stoughton.

Bryant, B. Harris, M. and Newton, D. (1980) in Davenport, G. C. (1994) *An Introduction to Child Development*. London: Harper Collins Publishers.

Carle, E. (1998) *The Very Busy Spider*. London: Hamish Hamilton.

Cousins, J. (11 July 1996) 'Hidden Treasure' in *Nursery World*, London.

Cousins, J. (18 July 1996) 'A Whole New World' in *Nursery World*, London.

Goldschmied, E. (1998) Telephone Conversation with B. Robb.

Leach, P. (1974) *Who Cares?*. London: Penguin.

Leach, P. (1994) *Children First*. London: Penguin.

Montessori, M. (1949) *The Absorbent Mind*. Madras, Adyar: Theosophical Publishing House.

Sylva, K., Roy C., Painter, M. (1980) *Child Watching at Playgroup and Nursery School*. London: Grant McIntyre.

Thornton, D. (September, 1997) 'All our children are special.' Seminar given at the *Nursery World* Early Years Conference, London.

Further reading

Allen, N. (1992) *Making Sense of the Children Act*. London: Longman Group.

Cattanch, A. (1991) *Working Together Under the Children Act*. London: HMSO.

Cattanch, A. (1993) *Play Therapy with Abused Children*. London: Kingsley Ltd.

5

Managing an Early Years Curriculum

This chapter looks at the curriculum for children under five years of age. Modern principles underlying the early childhood curriculum support a holistic view of the child as learner and an integrated approach to what is learned. Some pioneer workers in the field like Montessori and Froebel concentrated on developing the learning environment. Psychologists like Vygotsky and Bruner gave us theories of instruction with the adult as facilitator. Children learn through play and the best learning takes place when children are encouraged to be self-disciplined and autonomous. Observation, assessment and curriculum planning are based on what the child is able to do. Parents play an important role as their children's first educators. The early years curriculum is informed by the 'Desirable Outcomes for Children's Learning' and its quality is monitored by OFSTED inspections.

Curriculum definition

Curtis (1998) takes a broad view of what constitutes a curriculum. For her, the curriculum is:

> *everything that affects the child in the learning environment, overt and covert. It covers not only the activities, both indoors and outdoors, offered to young children, but the attitudes of the staff not only towards the children but to each other, to parents and anyone who visits the setting.*

Bruce and Meggitt (1996) represent the curriculum as a triangle with the **Child** at the apex and the **Content** and **Context** at opposite ends of the base. In their view:

Child involves knowledge and understanding about the **processes** of the child's development in the areas of language(s), play, and symbolic life as well as their spiritual, moral, emotional, social, intellectual and physical development.

Content consists of:

▶ what the child already knows
▶ what the child needs to know
▶ what the child wants to know.

Context consists of: people, culture, race, gender, special educational needs, access, materials and physical environment, outdoors, indoor places, events.

What both the above curriculum models hold in common is a holistic view of the child.

Principles of curriculum development

1 Childhood must be seen as valid in itself, as a part of life and not simply as preparation for adulthood. Thus education is for the present and not just a training for later.
2 The whole child is important. The emphasis is on physical and mental health as well as the importance of feelings, thinking and spirituality.
3 Learning is linked, not compartmentalised.
4 Intrinsic motivation, resulting in child initiated self-directed activity is valued.
5 Self-discipline is essential.
6 There are specially receptive periods of learning at different stages of development.
7 What children can do (rather than what they cannot do) is the starting point of a child's education.
8 The child has an inner life which emerges especially under favourable conditions.
9 The people (both adults and children) with whom the child interacts are of central importance.
10 The child's education is seen as an interaction between the child and the environment including in particular other people and knowledge itself.

The modern United Kingdom curriculum

In 1988, the Education Reform Act set out minimum requirements for a government-controlled curriculum (the National Curriculum) to be followed by children aged 5–16 years in state schools. The National

Curriculum has four key stages, Key stage 1 being followed by children aged 5–7 years.

The subjects taught in the National Curriculum are:

▶ Core subjects: English, mathematics and science.
▶ Foundation subjects: design and technology, information technology, history, geography, art, music, physical education.

The emphasis of the National Curriculum is on a 'top-down' approach to learning.

> *The National Curriculum is based upon an approach that assumes that every child should acquire certain knowledge and information, and concentrates upon what children are to become rather than upon what they are now.*
>
> (Curtis, 1998)

From the very outset, concerns were expressed that the National Curriculum would place 'downward pressure' upon children under statutory school age in mainstream education.

'Desirable Outcomes for Children's Learning'

In 1996, with the publication of the *Desirable Outcomes for Children's Learning on entering compulsory education* (see Chapter 9), learning 'guidelines' were set out for children under statutory school age in **six** areas of learning:

1 Personal and Social Development
2 Language and Literacy
3 Mathematics
4 Knowledge and Understanding of the World
5 Physical Development
6 Creative Development

Like the National Curriculum, the 'Desirable Outcomes' are subject based and 'in many ways inappropriate to young children's learning; although they are guidelines, not programmes of study' (Curtis, 1998). It is the aim of the 'Desirable Outcomes' that learning for the under-fives 'should lead into the National Curriculum programmes of study' (OFSTED, 1996). At a stroke, nursery education was brought under the influence of the National Curriculum. More recently, a publication from the DfEE mentions a 'policy for the education of three year olds . . . with targets for provision from 1999–2000 onwards' (*Early Years Development Partnerships and Plans*, 1998).

Common principles underpinning children's learning

Historically, early years educators have sought to make a distinction between the aims of nursery education and those of the rest of education. The Rumbold Committee advised in 1990 that:

> *The educator working with under-fives must pay careful attention not just to the content of the child's learning, but also to the way in which that learning is offered to and experienced by the child, and the role of all those involved in the process. Children are affected by the **context** in which learning takes place, the **people** involved in it and the **values and beliefs** which are embedded in it.*

In the wake of the 'Desirable Outcomes' and concerned about the changes being imposed by the government, the Early Childhood Education Forum drew up the following set of common principles to underpin early childhood education:

▶ Learning begins at birth.
▶ Care and education are inseparable – quality care is educational and quality education is caring.
▶ Every child develops at his or her own pace, but adults can stimulate and encourage learning.
▶ All children benefit from developmentally appropriate practice and education.
▶ Skilled and careful observations are the keys to helping children learn.
▶ Cultural and physical diversity should be respected and valued: a proactive anti-bias approach should be adopted and stereotypes challenged.
▶ Learning is holistic and cannot be compartmentalised: trust, motivation, interest, enjoyment and physical and social skills are as important as purely cognitive gains.
▶ Young children learn best through play, first-hand experience and talk.
▶ Carers and educators should work in partnership with parents, who are their children's first educators.
▶ Quality care and education require well-trained educators/carers and ongoing training and support.
(*Early Childhood Education Forum 1997, Curtis, 1998*).

Curtis observes that:

> *These principles support a process model of curriculum rather than the traditional model of education with its emphasis on subject knowledge and the implication*

that we know what subject knowledge children need in order to live in the next century.
(1998, page 19).

Planning a curriculum based on the 'Desirable Outcomes'

The School Curriculum and Assessment Authority (SCAA) specifies that the curriculum for children under statutory school age should be 'broad, balanced and purposeful' and should enable children 'to make maximum progress towards the Desirable Outcomes'. Plans should:

▶ be based on and extend what children already know and can do;
▶ demonstrate how individual aspects of planned learning relate to several curriculum areas;
▶ ensure that opportunities exist across the learning spectrum to encourage children's development: social, cultural, moral, spiritual;
▶ be weighted towards the areas of language and literacy, mathematics, and personal and social development;
▶ provide for the individual learning needs of all children, including children with special educational needs, children with English as an additional language and gifted children;
▶ value and provide for cultural differences and equal opportunities;
▶ consider the time factor in timetabling, teaching and learning in the long, medium and short term;
▶ help individual children to make progress in all six areas of learning.

Long-term planning

One effective method for managing long-term planning is to relate your permanent areas of provision to the 'Desirable Outcomes for Children's Learning'. Records of what children can learn in each of the areas of provision could be displayed near each area so that carers can see at a glance what children should be gaining from basic play provision. Lists of other resources that could be available in each area could also be displayed; for example items such as pens, paper, telephones, travel brochures, airline tickets, travel booking forms to encourage literacy in the home corner. Careful long-term planning will provide an ongoing structure of provision which requires only occasional updating.

Medium-term planning

This enables carers to decide what learning they intend to present to the children during the school or nursery term. It must take into consideration children's current interests and enthusiasms. It may include seasonal events such as a festival and special experiences such as an outing.

Staff must plan as a team, discussing and pooling ideas, which might be recorded on the spot during planning meetings. A useful tool for this might be a topic web from which individual themes, activities and learning can be developed later. From a comprehensive topic on 'Growing', for example, the theme 'Basic needs of Plants' might be explored.

From their ongoing programme of reviewing children's progress carers will have identified a number of learning priorities that need to be addressed during the coming term. These learning priorities will be drawn from all the six areas of learning. They may be for individual children or small or large groups. These learning priorities will form part of carers' intentions for children's learning. Forward planning is essential not only to ensure a balanced curriculum but also to enable carers to collect resources, do necessary research, inform parents and arrange for special experiences such as visits.

Short-term planning

When long-term and medium-term plans are in place, short-term plans can be completed efficiently. These outline in greater detail how learning will be presented on a day to day basis and may be targeted at an individual child, large or small groups. They will take into account children's interests and previous learning. They will identify areas of learning to be covered.

It is useful to have a system for recording short-term plans which is specific to your setting. This should include space for writing down:

1 Learning Intentions
2 Activity (a brief description)
3 Resources needed
4 Number of children (sometimes named) involved
5 Adult involvement
6 Language (possible questions, vocabulary)
7 Evaluation

It must be stressed that this is only a plan of intended learning. Carers must capitalise on spontaneous opportunities for children's learning which may arise from their curiosity or interest. Additional, unplanned learning should be recorded.

EXAMPLE

Carers at the village playgroup decided that the long-term aim of
developing children's knowledge and understanding of the world needed
to be emphasised. In their medium-term planning for the spring term
they chose to focus on the aim of encouraging children to look closely at
similarities, differences and change in the natural world. They planned
activities around the theme of 'Growing', using the subheadings, 'Frogs'
'Ourselves' and 'Plants'. At least two activities per week were planned
for the eleven-week term. Some activities (e.g. measuring and recording
growth) spanned the entire term. The following diagram illustrates the
progress of the term's work from long-term aims, through medium-term
aims to specific activities.

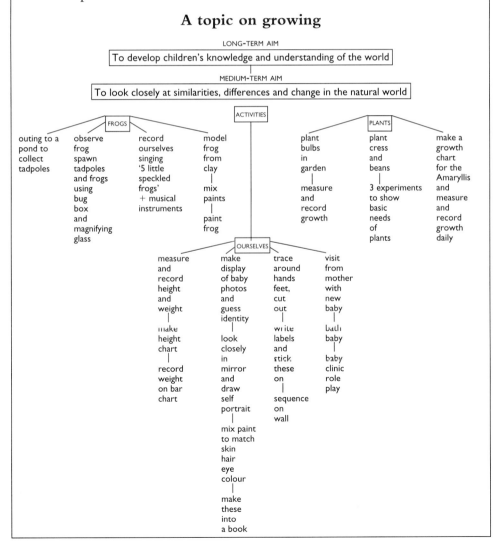

A topic on growing

LONG-TERM AIM

To develop children's knowledge and understanding of the world

MEDIUM-TERM AIM

To look closely at similarities, differences and change in the natural world

FROGS

outing to a pond to collect tadpoles

observe frog spawn tadpoles and frogs using bug box and magnifying glass

record ourselves singing '5 little speckled frogs' + musical instruments

model frog from clay
│
mix paints
│
paint frog

ACTIVITIES

PLANTS

plant bulbs in garden
│
measure and record growth

plant cress and beans
│
3 experiments to show basic needs of plants

make a growth chart for the Amaryllis and measure and record growth daily

OURSELVES

measure and record height and weight
│
make height chart
│
record weight on bar chart

make display of baby photos and guess identity
│
look closely in mirror and draw self portrait
│
mix paint to match skin hair eye colour
│
make these into a book

trace around hands feet, cut out
│
write labels and stick these on
│
sequence on wall

visit from mother with new baby
│
bath baby
│
baby clinic role play

The aims of planning in childminding

For younger children in the care of childminders, long-term planning depends upon a sound working knowledge of child development. The aim of the planning should be to develop each child's social, linguistic and motor skills through a graduated approach. Medium-term plans might target the development from large motor skills to small manipulative skills. Most of the planning for young children on an individual basis will be short-term. Planning must take into consideration the current state of health, likes and dislikes, and stage of development of each individual child. The child who is cared for in a childminder's home, in the company of other children and the childminder's own family, will learn from a range of social and linguistic exchanges. Young children learn most effectively by actively exploring and experimenting. Careful observation of children at play will enable childminders to provide appropriately challenging toys and activities for those in their charge. Most childminders write ad hoc notes on changes in a child's development to share with parents when the child is collected. If these observations are kept in individual notebooks, they form the basis of a shared child assessment programme involving the carer and the parents in partnership. This, in turn, informs future planning.

EXAMPLE

Mehmet, aged two, has recently been placed with his childminder, Carol. In her initial assessment, Carol observed that Mehmet is using an inferior pincer grasp (i.e. opposing whole first finger and whole thumb) to pick up jigsaw pieces. Her long-term aim is to promote Mehmet's physical development. Her medium-term aim is to develop Mehmet's fine manipulative skills. Her short-term aim is to encourage Mehmet's development from inferior to mature pincer grasp (i.e. opposing pads of first finger and thumb). Her short-term plan includes the following staged activities:

▶ building a tower with Duplo bricks;
▶ building a tower with Sticklebricks;
▶ building a tower with large Lego bricks;
▶ picking up large wooden beads;
▶ picking up smaller wooden beads;
▶ threading large wooden beads;
▶ threading smaller wooden beads.

Observation and assessment

Observations are the most natural means of knowing children in your care. Observation is only worthwhile if you make time to observe and focus on the individual child. Observation is an important aspect of your role as carer manager. It gives you the opportunity to assess:

- **ability** – absorb information about children's abilities, individual characteristics and areas of development;
- **progress** – be alert to children's progress, achievements or regression;
- **response** – observe reactions, 'what has the child gained?' and responses to given situations; make plans for future activities;
- **interests** – gain insight into the child's experiences and interests;
- **interaction** – look at groups, relationships and behaviour;
- **difficulties** – notice the beginning of problems.

Record-keeping

Types of record-keeping commonly used in early years settings are checklists, target-child observations and narrative. Photographs, videos and samples of children's work are also kept.

While checklists may be quick and easy for carers to use, they have certain disadvantages. Items included in the lists may take on a greater importance than those which are left out. Indeed, there is a real danger that they will come to be regarded as 'norms' and will form a basis for curriculum planning. Target-child observations, as described by Sylva, Roy and Painter (1980), can be somewhat mechanistic and strict adherence to timings can get in the way of child-watching. Narrative records, although somewhat cumbersome, are perhaps the most useful records of observations.

Involvement of parents

Parental participation in the assessment process is most important. The parent can provide you with background information which could include:

- Medical history
- Family situation
- Religious faith
- Dietary requirements
- Home language if not English
- Position in the family
- Likes and dislikes.

Your understanding and respect for this information is important for the settling-in of the child into the placement. You have to foster parent–carer dialogue if you are to get an holistic picture of the child. This principle is laid down in the Children Act 1989. Parents, at every opportunity, must be encouraged to be involved with their child's care and education. It is this partnership with parents that forms a key feature of the inspection process outlined in Chapter 9.

Involvement of children

You can discover what the child is capable of if you allow the child to participate actively in the assessment. Children seek and need adult attention. Through informal discussions, games and simple questions you can quickly establish 'where the child is at'. If you want to empower children you have to let them contribute to their assessment and thereby recognise and respect their individuality, encourage their efforts and value their opinions. If you have ever been appraised or reviewed you will surely know how valued you felt when you were able to participate actively in the process.

Evaluation

Kerr's (1968) model of evaluation is far too complex to be described in detail but in essence it looks at ways of assisting the carer to refine the learning process. Evaluation therefore is not solely about examining how much the child has absorbed but looking at the factors which have influenced performance. Evaluation is an ongoing repeated process of curriculum design.

Evaluation gives you an insight into what the child actually assimilates or takes up. According to the activity, you can assess what was useful or not. What you are offering, the child they may not be receiving. Does this mismatch depend on how the curriculum is being offered?

The manager's role in curriculum delivery

The carer manager's role in curriculum delivery is: to work as the leader of a team in planning and organising a learning environment which is sufficiently challenging and stimulating to stretch the most able children and is secure enough for the most timid;

- to supervise provision of suitable and adequate resources and materials to enable the curriculum to function both indoors and outdoors;
- to act as facilitator supporting and directing each child's learning skills and competencies;
- to ensure that the day to day routines and activities encourage a child's independence of thought and action by enabling the child to own and control their environment;
- to support and extend children's language and through high level verbal and non-verbal interactions;
- to keep detailed individual records based on observations of children and assessment of their future needs and special needs;
- to ensure that carers have a knowledge of child development and a wide range of skills including interpersonal skills.

Theories of early years curriculum

Is the education provided in early childhood effective? Does it harm the child's early development? Can it harm the relationship of pre-school children with their families? The short answer is that one study showed that high quality early childhood education for disadvantaged children is a highly effective way of improving their life chances (Hohmann, Banet and Wickar, 1979).

Maria Montessori

Maria Montessori (1870–1952), an Italian doctor, is one of the pioneers of nursery education. At the beginning of the century she developed her ideas about teaching young children through working with children who had learning difficulties. Her conclusions from studying and teaching children, mostly from deprived backgrounds, were that children 'unfolded' regardless of environment, given the proper stimulation and the proper materials. Montessori pioneered the idea that children do not need to be forced. She believed that all children go through certain stages of development, linked to certain types of learning. She designed special learning materials and equipment to mesh with the sequential stages. Montessori suggested that teachers and older children act as mentors in shaping the younger child's innate abilities. Montessori believed that each child has to be free to learn and develop according to their individual physiological and psychological needs. Learning can only occur in a specifically prepared environment designed to develop the child's intellectual potential through stimulation and refinement of the senses. The environment will promote a positive attitude to learning and develop a general feeling of competence in the child's daily activities.

THE MONTESSORI MODEL

This model of pre-school education uses spacious colourful classrooms arranged in an orderly way. Montessori's theory on the absorbent mind and sensitive periods of development led her to devise and arrange a specially prepared environment for learning to take place. There are low tables and chairs, visible shelves within reach with everything in a specific place and individual working rugs for each child. Order, organisation and classification are very important as they help create clear and orderly thinking. Children from 3–5 years work individually or in small groups usually helped by older children. Younger children learn from observing older children. The children select the desired material to work with and take it to their workplace or mat. When the children have finished they return the material to its proper place. The Montessori atmosphere is of quiet activity and long periods of concentration in the child's chosen activity. Apart from easel painting there are no special art activities nor dramatic play. The child moves about in an atmosphere that respects them as an individual. The child teaches him or herself in response to interest, free to choose any appropriate material in any area. The teacher or directoress prepares herself and the learning environment. The directoress demonstrates the learning materials to the child. She observes the child carefully and decides what materials to offer and when.

Self-selection and accomplishment lead to inner control and self-mastery. Most of the materials are self-correcting, so that the child can learn from mistakes. Montessori believed that a child should be involved with his or her environment from birth as far as possible. The first six years are seen as a vital period of development as during this time the child inevitably learns particular skills and concepts. These are for example: walking, language, development of particular senses, love of order. Montessori stressed that children should work at their own pace and not that of the adults.

MONTESSORI MATERIALS

1 Tools to foster competence
  Frames with pieces of fabric or leather attached that can be buttoned, hooked, tied together, zipped and joined in many ways. The child learns to dress and undress him or herself and learns a feeling of competence, a sense of independence. They also become competent in their environment: cleaning, washing surfaces, putting away materials, polishing shoes, preparing vegetables, serving food, washing dolls, arranging flowers and so on.

2 Tools to develop sensory skills
  Montessori assumed that intelligence has sensori-motor roots which can be developed through sensory interaction with the environment. She developed sets of learning materials based on what she had used for children with special needs. These were known as didactic apparatus and were designed to enable children to correct themselves by trial and error.
    There are didactic materials such as:

  ▶ blocks of wood with easily removed cylinder inserts of different sizes for sorting, geometric shapes to build a tower;
  ▶ wooden prisms of different sizes which can be arranged in thickness;
  ▶ tactile materials, smooth and fine which can be identified blindfold;
  ▶ auditory objects with distinct sounds;
  ▶ sets of smelling bottles.

  Children are encouraged not to run in the classroom and to work calmly and quietly at all times. A bell may be sounded to tell the children that it is time to be silent.

3 Tools to teach academic skills
  Montessori's prime aim was to teach children to be independent, strong willed, clear minded and able to concentrate and persevere and be sensitive to things around them so that everything would be of interest or value. She devised special materials to prepare the children for learning the 3Rs which she believed would follow from their minds and hands becoming attuned. Metal geometric shapes or insets are used by the children for design and as a preparation for writing.

Friedrich Froebel (1782–1852)

Froebel, a German educator, founded his first kindergarten in 1840. He believed that children need to be physically active outdoors as well as indoors. In the *garten*, children played active games, studied natural science and experienced freedom of movement.

Froebel put great importance on play, particularly symbolic play, and encouraged children to pretend and use their imagination. He maintained that play encourages thinking. Froebel's ideas on education form the basis of modern curricula. He introduced his pupils to literature, singing, rhyme, finger plays, arts and crafts. He believed that parents are a child's primary educators. Froebel encouraged free-flow play and children's relationships with one another.

Froebel designed what he called 'gifts' and 'occupations'. His first gift consisted of 6 soft balls, the second of a wooden ball, a cylinder and a cube. Cuboids, rods, triangles and prisms followed. These were the tools of mathematical tracking. Occupations were the crafts: drawing, collage making, modelling with clay.

Lev Vygotsky (1896–1935)

Vygotsky was a Russian psychologist who studied children's learning in the 1920s and 1930s. He presumed that a child's level of ability is not represented by what they can do alone, but by what they can do with help. Vygotsky believed that the gap which exists between what children know and can do alone and what they can do with someone or others more knowledgeable and accomplished than themselves is very important. Vygotsky used the phrase **zone of actual development** to define what a child can do at a given moment. This Vygotsky believed to be the result of previous learning. He used the phrase **zone of proximal or potential development** to describe tasks which the child might be unable to perform alone but could do with help.

Vygotsky believed that social interaction and communication are essential tools of cognitive development. His research showed that children could learn much from each other. The role of the adult is to collaborate with the child in his learning, sharing and facilitating understanding. The adult must provide a challenging and stimulating environment, focusing on the child's next step, careful not to confront the child with too much that is new. Vygotsky stressed the importance of play. Through pretend play, children can do things they cannot manage in real life. Play helps the child consolidate what they learn.

Jerome Bruner (1915–)

Bruner, an American psychologist, through his Theory of Cognitive Development and Theories of Instruction, has informed attitudes to early years curriculum in Britain. Jerome Bruner believes that adults can be a great help to children in their thinking by supporting their experiences. Bruner's theory of infant skill development has the following features:

THEORY OF COGNITIVE DEVELOPMENT

Bruner divided cognitive development into modes of thinking which 'translate experiences into a model of the world'.

His three modes for children's learning are as follows:

1 **Enactive mode** – learning
   Children learn through first-hand active experiences. This is how young children first learn. Bruner called this 'a mode of representing past events through appropriate motor responses'. Children need to move about and to have real, first-hand direct experiences. This helps their ideas and their thought processes to develop.
2 **Iconic mode** – imagining
   Children can imagine what they learn. This learning depends on sight and the other senses. Internalised images stand for objects and experiences. In Bruner's terms, this mode provides 'a visual path or pattern' which is recognisable. Children need to be reminded of their prior experiences; books and interest tables with objects displayed on them are useful aids to this recall of prior experience.
3 **Symbolic mode** – transferring
   Children have the ability to transfer what they learn into symbolic codes. Children represent learning in language and symbols. These codes are important: music, mathematics, drawing, painting, dance and play are all useful codes to represent learning which Bruner call symbolic thinking. This abstract learning emerges from about seven years of age. Modes emerge in sequence, continue to function interactively throughout life and are dominant at different times.

   Adults confronted with a new task, such as learning how to operate a computer, may have to pass through **enactive** and **ionic** modes. Bruner explains that even a learner who has a well developed symbolic system may lack the imagery to resort to in solving a particular problem. Therefore his symbolic transformations prove inadequate. Bruner's Theory of Cognitive Development interacts with his Theories of Instruction.

Laura, aged three and a half, had been drawing people for six months. With the addition of a new symbol (a nose) she created a pig: an example of symbolic thinking

THEORIES OF INSTRUCTION

1 **Spiral curriculum** Bruner argued that 'any subject can be taught to any child at any stage if it is presented in an intellectually honest form' (Curtis, 1998). In other words, aspects of literature, mathematics, history, geography and science can be made accessible to any child at the appropriate level for their stage and age of development. Bruner believes that the learning process can be accelerated by adopting this spiral approach to the curriculum. Bruner implies that unless activities and experiences that adults plan to offer children can be related to future learning, they have no place in the curriculum.

2 **Scaffolding** In his writing, Bruner places great emphasis on the role of the adult in children's learning. The adult is the provider of a stimulating environment which encourages discovery. More importantly, the adult

plays an active collaborative role by providing a supportive structure (scaffold) for children's learning. At the beginning of the learning experience the child needs support but as the child gains competence and confidence, the scaffolding can be gradually removed until the child is in control and the scaffold is no longer needed.

Through skilful observation of the learning child and careful assessment of the child's learning, the informed adult will know when the child is ready for the next step in the learning structure. This notion of scaffolding is very similar to the Russian psychologist Vygotsky's idea of the zone of proximal development.

At the beginning of the learning experience the child needs adult support

Further approaches to early years curriculum

FREE FLOW PLAY

This type of play happens spontaneously. It occurs when children are most deeply involved in play and are concentrating totally. The role of the adult is to ensure that children's play is undisturbed. This is the type of play which benefits from sensitive offers of props or verbal input to extend the play and keep it going. Carers need to be on the lookout for free flow play so that they can act quickly to help to keep the play going if it appears to be faltering. Direct adult intervention can stop free flow play dead. Indirect intervention is best.

HIGH-SCOPE CURRICULUM

This structured programme was developed in the USA in the 1960s and 1970s, based on work with deprived children. It closely involved parents in children's learning. Its aim was to prepare children for future schooling. The High-Scope curriculum is based on the assumption that children are active learners and that they learn best from programmes which they devise and implement by themselves. It makes children responsible for their own learning. They must work to a 'Plan-Do-Review' routine. They inform an adult of their plan, carry it out, then discuss the outcome of their learning with the adult. The success of the programme depends on close observation of children, extensive record-keeping, partnership with parents, individual learning programmes and a high level of adult–child communication. The programme is criticised because of the lack of direct adult involvement at the planning stage and its rigid structure.

ACTIVITIES

After reading this chapter you may like to complete some of the following activities.

1. DRAW UP MEDIUM-TERM PLANS OVER THREE WEEKS BASED ON A RELIGIOUS FESTIVAL.

You may find it helpful to consider the following:

▶ Involvement of parents.
▶ Relationship to 'Desirable Learning Outcomes' (DLOs).
▶ Learning needs of two to three children.

2. CARRY OUT A TARGET CHILD ASSESSMENT.

▶ Look at this child's task.
▶ Assess this child's language.
▶ Look at his activity record.
▶ Note the programme followed at time of observation.

3. EVALUATE A WEEKLY PROGRAMME YOU CARRIED OUT WITH A NUMBER OF CHILDREN.

▶ Which DLOs provide specific focus for the learning?
▶ What evidence is there of children's learning?
▶ Examine the use of resources.

References

Bruce, T. and Meggitt, C. (1996) *Child Care and Education*. London: Hodder & Stoughton.

Curtis, A. (1998) *A Curriculum for the Pre-School Child*. London: Routledge.

DES Rumbold Report (1990) *Starting with Quality*. London: HMSO.

DfEE and SCAA (1996) *Nursery Education: Desirable Outcomes for Children's Learning*. Sudbury: DfEE Publications Centre.

DfEE and SCAA (1996) *Nursery Education Scheme: The Next Steps*. Sudbury: DfEE Publications Centre.

DfEE (1998) *Early Years Development Partnerships and Plans*. Sudbury: DfEE Publications Centre.

Hohmann, M., Banet, B. and Wickhart, D. (1979) *Young Children in Action*. London: High-Scope Press.

Kerr, S. (1968) *Ultimate Rewards: What Really Motivates People to Achieve?* New York: Harvard Business School.

Sylva, K., Roy, C. and Painter, M. Child (1980) *Watching at Playgroup and Nursery School*. London: Grant McIntyre

Further reading

Gura, P. (1992) *Exploring Learning*. London: Paul Chapman Ltd.

Hobart, C. and Frankl, J. (1994) *Child Observation*. London: Stanley Thornes.

SCAA (1997) *Looking at Children's Learning*. London: School Curriculum Assessment Authority.

Managing Children's Behaviour

This chapter sets out chronologically the expectations for behaviour in young children. It offers strategies for managing challenging behaviour and suggests the positive social skills that children can acquire. The chapter discusses assessment of children's behaviour and outlines the Staged Process for children with special educational needs. Included are several psychological models of behaviour that are applicable to the early years setting.

Accepting children as they are

Stages and cycles of the child

The child carer could be responsible for a child as young as a few months and as old as five years. Eighty per cent of the children in your care will exhibit acceptable behaviour and 20 per cent of children will present challenging behaviour. Following the same ratio the 20 per cent who are a challenge will take up 80 per cent of your time and energy.

Behaviour changes with age and child behaviour appears in cycles:

Cycles in children's behaviour

Age of child			Behaviour
2 years	5 years	10 years	smooth, consolidated
2½	5–6	11 years	breaking up
3	6½	12 years	rounded, balanced
3½	7	13 years	inward looking
4	8	14	vigorous, expansive
4½	9	15	inward–outward looking
			troubled, neurotic
5	10	16	smooth, consolidated

Source: Francis Ilg and Louise Bates Ames (1996)

Linking stages of development to age can be unreliable. The order in which behaviour appears is more significant than when exactly it occurs. As a carer manager you will find that your levels of acceptance or non-acceptance of challenging behaviour will largely depend on the situation and the age of the child. The term 'terrible twos', for example, conditions adults to tolerate certain behaviour from a two year old that would not be acceptable at a later stage of development.

What behaviour can the carer expect at different ages?

0–12 MONTHS

The first year in a child's life is the beginning of their self-awareness. Physically the child begins to distinguish the 'me' from the not 'me'. The child will discover and explore their own body. Psychologically, the child learns from actions and reactions of others about self-worth and self-value. The loved, nurtured and respected child will develop in a balanced way physically and emotionally.

12–24 MONTHS

At 18 months 'no' is the child's favourite word and doing the opposite to what they are told now becomes their most enjoyable diversion. Life is in the present. There is only NOW. The child's interpersonal relationships are completely dominated by **taking** rather than **giving**. Parents, or carers, may be treated as things to be pulled, stepped and climbed on. However, by two years old the child shows more patience and will share and be loveable and affectionate.

TWO YEARS OLDS

At around two and a half years old children can become a challenge as temperamentally they are not an easy, adaptable member of any social group. This is the peak age of disequilibrium. The two and a half year old is rigid and inflexible; wanting what they want when they want it. Time is NOW and their routine is dominant. The child is domineering and demanding. 'Me do it!' is the favourite phrase.

This is the age of extremes when **want** and **don't want** are in constant conflict. Because there is no past or future, anything the child does must go on for ever, whether this is playing or having a story read.

THREE YEARS OLD

At three years old, the child learns that 'yes' also gets action. They will be ready to share once more and now use the royal 'we' to express their cooperative, easy-going attitude to life. There is more balance in their life, both towards adults and towards things around them. Rituals and routine are no longer so important. The three year old no longer demands that things be done his way; he will even enjoy doing things your way.

The age of three and a half, however, brings a tremendous change as if in order to reach the balance usual at age five they now have to break up and then consolidate. The child of three and a half will be insecure, unbalanced and lacking coordination. Not only will there be fear of heights, falling and stumbling, but also stuttering. A child's inner tension may express itself in blinking, biting his nails, picking his nose and thumb sucking. There may be relationship difficulties; a child may question whether the carer loves him. He once again wants complete attention.

FOUR YEARS OLD

At four years old the child reaches an out of bounds stage of development when they hit, kick, break things and run away. The four year old is loud and talkative. Behaviour ranges from silly laughter to profanity. There is defiance of authority, swaggering, boasting and children will defy even threats of actual punishment. The line between truth and untruths becomes blurred and fiction becomes more interesting than fact. As a child progresses to five he is beginning to sort out the real from the make believe.

At four and a half years old, children are more self-motivated and persevering, finishing what they start. Their emerging reading skills may lead to endless discussions and questions but equally they will want to draw and be interested in letters and numbers.

FIVE YEARS OLD

Five years old sees a return to equilibrium as the child becomes reliable, stable and well adjusted – and normally is ready for the transition from pre-school care to regular school.

Meeting the challenge

From the above it can be seen that every child at every age can be challenging. Usually they dispute adult values and perspectives; this behaviour may be related to a particular age or cycle but its expression is fairly consistent:

▶ Resistance, defiance, rebellion, negativism
▶ Resentment, anger, hostility
▶ Aggression, retaliation, striking back
▶ Lying, hiding, fleeing.

Approaches to the challenge

Psychologists have categorised the approaches used by carers using the following terminology. Although these categories describe tendencies in carers they are of course simplistic.

THE ALL POWERFUL CARER

This approach demands unquestioning obedience. Such obedience is not open to negotiation. The child, denied the element of choice, is also denied responsibility. The child who is always instructed what to do will not develop judgement, initiative or independence.

THE AUTHORITATIVE CARER

This approach is more helpful to the child. It is a better approach to caring because it is responsive, yet communicates clearly a desire for mature, controlled behaviour. There are rules but there are also expressed reasons: where there is participation, there is motivation. The child is more likely to agree with the reason for doing something, if they feel that they have had some part in the decision making. Authoritative caring teaches the child skills to resolve conflict and challenge authority. When reasons behind the need for action are expressed, feelings are also expressed.

> ### EXAMPLE
>
> Anna had to be forced to go to pre-school every morning. When asked why she was reluctant to go she replied, 'I'm afraid you might forget to pick me up again'. Once Anna was reassured that her mother would soon return she went off willingly.

THE PERMISSIVE CARER

This approach gives little direction and makes few demands on the child with the result that children are less self-reliant and less self-controlled.

THE HARMONIOUS CARER

This approach still exerts control but the carer seldom needs to use it. The children do what the carers wish without adult intervention. For example, this type of control is effective where the children are compliant by nature, happily involved in their play and concentrating intently.

THE NON-CONFORMIST CARER

This approach offers a principled set of values emphasising the need to allow the child to develop freely. This model of caring is more structured than permissive caring and produces more competent children than those of permissive carers, but makes it difficult for the child to fit in later to society.

Strategies for managing challenging behaviour

TEACHING LIMITS

There are rules that have to be understood and obeyed for the safety and well-being of the individual and society. Toddlers begin to learn that there are limits in life and that rules continue. The approach to the challenging child has to be consistent; whatever is prohibited will always be so. Inconsistency leads the child to believe that it is a game and they will either test the limits or get confused about the message.

EXAMPLE

Abdul, aged three, has a compulsive desire to pick up stones from the gravel path. More often than not, he throws them. His key worker, Usha, is consistent in discouraging Abdul's behaviour. She makes it quite clear that picking up stones is unacceptable in the following circumstances:

- ▶ 'Abdul, we don't pick up stones. They're needed on the path.'
- ▶ 'We don't throw stones: it's dangerous. Someone might get hurt.'
- ▶ 'Please don't put stones down the slide. Someone might land on them and be hurt.'
- ▶ 'If you put stones on the trampoline, they'll end up on the lawn and damage the mower. The gardener will be cross.'
- ▶ 'No, we don't put stones on the lawn either. Please pick them up.'
- ▶ 'Please take those stones out of your pocket and put them back on the path.'
- ▶ 'Please dump those stones out of the boot of the car. They belong on the path.'

Usha realises that her consistency has paid off when she overhears Abdul say to his twin sister, 'You mustn't pick up stones.'

BE SPECIFIC

It is important to state the rule and the reason behind it rather than just saying 'No'.

EXAMPLE

'Do not pull the cat's tail because it hurts.' Although it is frustrating to be continually asked 'why', the easy option of 'because I told you so' teaches the child nothing.

REMOVE THE CHILD — TIME OUT

Sometimes children will not respond to reason. In this case the best tactic is simply to remove the contested object or the unreasonable child from the situation. This is a technique described by Dr. Christopher Green, which he calls 'Time Out'. The aim of Time Out is to provide a cooling off period for adult and child when they become locked into an escalating conflict destined to end in stalemate. The method is to remove the child to another room for a short time. The intended result is that both parties will calm down, regain their composure and emerge with their dignity intact. The child should not be expected to apologise but rather return in a more reasonable mood. As a management technique, Time Out should be used sparingly, as a last resort when all other strategies and diplomacies have failed.

EXAMPLE

David arrived at the daycare centre in a tantrum because Mum had forgotten his favourite teddy at home. Several children offered him their own soft toys for the morning. Their offers were rebuffed with flailing arms and the owner of a particularly attractive Dalmatian was kicked. David was gently but firmly removed to an unexciting resources room. In this case, the door was left open. The other children, upset by his anger, piled soft toys in the doorway. Gradually, David emerged, calmed by his exclusion and joined the group in imaginative play with a 'vet' theme.

USE SENSIBLE TIMING

It is pointless asking a child who is not physically or mentally ready to comply with your wishes. For example, a two year old cannot be expected to sit still and listen to a long story.

TEACH GRADUALLY

Most children will cooperate if they are introduced to a behaviour with patience and sensitivity. A child needs time to adjust so rushing is self-defeating. Each child has his or her own pace for learning and practising new behaviours.

EXAMPLE

Four-year-old Leela is excited. It is news time. She has a surprise. It is her new puppy, Fedo. Leela wants to tell the group of all her week-end adventures with Fedo. Leela is irrepressible. When others are giving their news Leela keeps interrupting. Her carer recognises her enthusiasm and gently reminds Leela that she has had her turn and must listen to the others.

Cross-cultural research supports Piaget's findings that intellectual development follows the same sequence of stages, though children develop at different ages. Therefore what one child might understand at age four may still puzzle another at age six.

USE POSITIVE REINFORCEMENT

Encouragement, smiles and genuine praise for cooperation produce positive results. These strategies lead to repetition of the desired behaviour because they build on children's needs for love and gratification. Scolding and yelling will not alter undesirable behaviour permanently.

EXAMPLE

Two-year-old Kim, totally absorbed with the wooden train set, continues to play though Nanny has said it is 'tidy-up-time'. Taking the toy box over to Kim, Nanny encourages her to part with the train set.

'We have to go to the book corner to hear your favourite story but we must tidy up first. Let's put the train away.' Kim puts one carriage reluctantly into the box. Immediately Nanny responds joyfully. Kim's action is followed by a positive response from Nanny. She is praised. This is repeated until the entire train set is put away. Research shows that social reinforcers, as in the above example, encourage the desired behaviour and are much more productive than shouting or screaming.

BE FIRM AND CONFIDENT

Be secure in your conviction that what you are asking is because you love the child and genuinely believe the behaviour to be the best. Indecision and inconsistency cause confusion.

> ## Example
>
> Beth pleaded with her Nanny, 'Please can we play with our toy soldiers at the table while we are having lunch'. Beth knew that during meals toys were left off the table but was hoping that with her friend Becky to lunch it would be different. Nanny, firm but gentle, reminded her of the rule they shared. Although there is usually room to be flexible, children respect consistency. It is much simpler for the child if there is a consistent policy of discipline, as the child can act confidently in the knowledge that you can be relied on to do as you say.

Avoid preaching and moralising

Telling a child they are bad or naughty attacks their self-worth and not their behaviour. Firm, gentle control is more successful than preaching. It is possible to judge a child's behaviour without devaluing her as a person.

> ## Example
>
> Three-year-old Zak was gleeful. The childminder Mrs Jones had to take Abdhu to the bathroom and at last Zak could play with the castle that Abdhu had carefully built. On returning to the lounge and seeing how Zak had altered his structure Abdhu screamed, took up a fire engine and threw it angrily at Zak's head. Screams and tears follow.
>
> Mrs Jones comforts Zak and reprimands Abdhu by saying: 'You are very naughty Abdhu. You are older and ought to know better. You should never have thrown the fire engine at Zak. You always react this way if someone else plays with your toys. You are horrible. You must never do this again!'
>
> It is important to try to understand the child's view. In this situation Zak had interfered with Abdhu's precious structure without his permission. Zak, on the other hand, could see a better way to arrange the castle wall and wanted to show Abdhu. Research suggests that if carers are insensitive to their points of view, children are less likely to understand the view points of others. Words such as should, ought, must, always and never are best avoided.
>
> Say instead, 'Abdhu, throwing the fire engine was a very naughty thing to do.' (It is the behaviour and not the child that is condemned.) 'Come and say sorry to Zak for throwing the fire engine at him.' (The child is encouraged to apologise for his behaviour.) 'Can we share in your game?' The adult seeks permission and bridges the gap.

TEACH ALTERNATIVES

Teach children what they may do as well as what they may not do. Stop a child writing on a wall but give them paper to express themself. Stop the child hitting another and encourage them to use polite language to express their feeling instead. Wherever possible show the child what you want them to do.

EXAMPLE

Three-year-old Simon, new to the playgroup, constantly snatched toys from other children. There were tears of frustration as Lucy reported, 'Simon has taken my helmet'. Simon with the helmet on his head was gently taken by the hand and led to Lucy by Mrs Bart. She stooped down between them. 'Simon I want you to give the helmet back to Lucy and ask for it nicely. What is the magic word? Yes, please. What do you say to Lucy now that she has kindly lent you the helmet?' Mrs Bart chose for music time the song 'Two Little Magic Words – please and thanks'. The children were able to act out the words.

USE DISTRACTIONS

Children need to learn that there are limits, but do not let a situation degenerate into a contest of wills, as with telling the child what not to do. Children will naturally prefer to continue what they are enjoying and may refuse to cooperate. Getting a child to do what you want requires tact and careful assessment of the situation. If the activity to be stopped is negative, then a distraction is far more effective than an outright veto.

EXAMPLE

Two-and-a-half-year-old Gavin finds a sharp knife and is eagerly attempting to cut a sheet of paper. 'Look Gavin if you use this pair of scissors you can cut the paper *and* make an interesting pattern. Shall I show you?' The carer demonstrates and produces a star much to Gavin's surprise. He is delighted. He pushes the knife away and wants to use the scissors to do the same.

IGNORE UNDESIRABLE BEHAVIOUR

You cannot ignore dangerous activities but some behaviours are better ignored. Temper tantrums become more common as young children grow more assertive. Temper tantrums are a child's way of establishing their independence and defending their self-image. The child becomes self-conscious. The child increasingly understands that they are separate from their parent and have choices. The child becomes angry and frustrated as many of their attempts to be independent fail. There is no one way of managing temper tantrums as each child and circumstance is different.

> **EXAMPLE**
>
> Leela returns from the morning session at the toddlers group very tired. Her Nanny realises that Leela needs to sleep. Leela is kicking and screaming as she wants to stay up. Leela will not be comforted. Nanny suggests that Leela screams in her room. Nanny carries Leela to her room and ignores her tantrums, busying herself in the next room.

TEACH A LOGICAL CONSEQUENCE TO BAD BEHAVIOUR

Negative consequences may be useful if the child can make the connection between the consequences and their actions.

> **EXAMPLE**
>
> Four-year-old Fergus repeatedly teased the parrot by rattling the cage and poking the bird with a stick. On one occasion Fergus lost his stick in the cage and squeezed his fingers through to retrieve it. The parrot seized one of his fingers fiercely and broke it. When questioned at the hospital Fergus admitted his misdemeanour. He subsequently told all his friends not to interfere with the parrot.

SCOLDING

This is acceptable when it tells the child, If you do that adults will get angry. Making an angry face and saying 'NO' can have the necessary effect. It is good practice frequently to remind children of the rules, the purpose for having rules and what will happen if the rules are broken.

> **EXAMPLE**
>
> It is outdoor play and all the children are happily playing correctly with the equipment provided. Megan comes swirling down the slide. It seems everyone wants to have a go on the slide. Megan is impatient for her

turn. She has another turn but this time she attempts to run up the slide as Kate is coming down. 'No, no that will NOT do!' The tone, pitch and severity of the words frighten Megan. She hurriedly says she is sorry. Megan cautions the other children, 'Don't run up the slide because Miss Blotts will be angry with you'.

DEPRIVATION

Take away the offending object or toy for a period of time.

EXAMPLE

Harry uses the track from the wooden train set as a gun. He chases the children around the room pretending to be a robber. Harry is most unhappy when the track is taken away. It is an essential piece of the rail track and Harry will have to wait until after lunch to play properly with the train set. His carer deprives him of his toy. After lunch the rail is returned to Harry. The carer makes no mention of the previous incident. The episode is over and the child is starting again.

PHYSICAL PUNISHMENT

▶ Spanking is **unacceptable**, even if the parent condones it and says you should.
▶ Physical punishment does not foster mutual respect
▶ Children will imitate what you do.
▶ Physical punishment does **not** develop the child's mind.
▶ Physical punishment does **not** tell the child why.

The behaviour policy

As with all other policies, the behaviour policy will be specific to each setting. It is important for children to share in the drawing up of this policy. If children feel that they 'own' the rules of the setting, they are less likely to break them. Rules should be few and simply expressed so that children can remember them easily and remind each other. Children's rules might include:

▶ Help each other
▶ Help take care of group property
▶ Adults are in charge
▶ Don't break the 'danger' rules
▶ Be kind, especially to younger and less able children.

Some groups have a 'never say you can't play' rule.

The skills children need

In the enabling environment where each individual is respected and their needs are met, children can be taught skills necessary to implement their behaviour policy. These are:

POLITENESS

Children will need to be encouraged and shown how to use words like 'please', 'thank you' and 'excuse me' in the new context of the setting. Social skills fit naturally into the serving and sharing of food.

SHARING

This may be a difficult concept for some children to learn, particularly as the word does not always imply equality: a child who has been encouraged to 'share' their sweets may be quite reluctant to relinquish the best tricycle in the room.

TAKING TURNS

Learning to take turns implies being at a stage of maturity where children can wait for their needs to be gratified. Helpful carers can sometimes make the waiting more bearable. Games involving very few children can help, as can turning the pages of the story book being read to a small group.

LEARNING TO NEGOTIATE

Carers may have to step in to help children to de-centre (see page 44) and appreciate that there are two sides in a dispute. By suggesting alternatives or encouraging cooperation, carers can teach children negotiating skills.

WHEN TO REFER

It may be necessary to refer children to psychologists or health professionals if the child's actions persist in being:

▶ **unpredictable** – child displays disturbing mood swings.
▶ **rebellious** to the extent that you as carer manager are unable to impose your authority or where the child appears unable to control his own behaviour.
▶ **not understandable**, that is, where the child's behaviour, attitudes or moods go against the norm and there seems to be a lack of reason or meaning.

Observation and recording of difficult behaviour

The learning expectations in the DfEE and SCAA publication *Desirable Outcomes for Children's Learning* may serve as a guide for observing and assessing a child's behaviour. In the case of behaviour which is causing concern, observations should be carried out regularly and systematically.

Stage I

Where observations seem to indicate that causes for concern about a child's behaviour might be physiological or psychological in nature, the parents must be informed of your suspicions. No further steps may be taken without the parent's consent and involvement. The parent may be able to add information which will help with the overall assessment of the child. At this stage, the child's name should be placed on the setting's SEN register. This is the first stage of the five stage process for assessing a child's special educational needs as set out by the *Code of Practice* (1994) published by the DfEE.

Detailed records of the child's behaviour will continue to be kept by both the setting and the parent. One good model for recording such behaviour is the 'ABC' method:

- ► A (antecedent)   What preceded the incident?
- ► B (behaviour)   What actually happened?
- ► C (consequence)   What reactions were generated by the behaviour?

Stage II

After six weeks, parents and staff get together to discuss whether concern still exists or whether action taken has been remedial. If there is still a problem, an Individual Education Plan of action is drawn up, entitled 'Stage II'. At this stage, parents should be encouraged to seek outside help from professionals such as the child's GP or health visitor. Social Services may also become involved at this stage if there are concerns over the child's welfare. The child, in extreme cases, might be on the Child Protection Register. Regular meetings with parents will continue every six to twelve weeks to review progress.

Stage III

If there is no progress, professional help will be sought with parental consent. The child will be assessed by an educational psychologist. This is

Stage III. If there is progress, then the child will move back to Stage II. Early Years settings are rarely involved at Stages IV or V.

Managing feelings

Children experience very strong emotions and alternate rapidly from positive to negative feelings. One of your tasks as carer manager is to help children to achieve a balance between emotional extremes. Erikson's theory will give you an insight into children's feelings.

Erikson's developmental stages

Erik H. Erikson (1902–94) devised a theory of the eight developmental stages of man based on Sigmund Freud's Psychodynamic Theory of Personality. Erikson believed that a child has to go through several stages to come into adult society. The child must resolve dilemmas and find ways to harmonise competing goals and purposes which pull in opposing directions. Erikson himself says:

> *Children, 'fall apart' repeatedly and, unlike Humpty Dumpty, grow together again.*

The table below gives an indication of the balances that must be struck in childhood.

Erikson's developmental stages

	Stage	Task	Subjective experience
I	INFANCY Trust	 To get	Secure; sure of self; trusting in the world; expecting the best from others; certain that difficulties can be met and pain relieved; having faith and hope in life
	vs	vs	vs
	Mistrust	To give in return	Mistrust; apprehension; uncertainty; fear; ambiguity; feeling that life is very risky, painful, chaotic
II	EARLY CHILDHOOD Autonomy	 To hold on	Independent; able to manage oneself; aware of own strengths; confident; sturdy; resourceful; self-reliant; curious; able to meet others' demands; able to make choices on basis of one's own preference
	vs	vs	vs
	Shame; Doubt	To let go	Ashamed; doubting; exposed; surprised; inadequate; caught off guard; powerless; helpless; dependent

	Stage	Task	Subjective experience
III	ACTIVE PLAY AGE		Able to channel energy; showing self-control; can hold self in check; able to express enthusiasm and exuberance constructively; others pleased to see me coming; lively and expansive; able to question rules and to challenge authority freely, openly, directly without losing control of self
	Initiative	To go after	
	vs	vs	vs
	Guilt	To play like	Guilty; hostile; aggressive; out of control; hurting; breaking; getting carried away
IV	SCHOOL AGE		Competent; productive; capable; can take things in stride; having energy that flows freely into planned activities; can see something through to completion, showing pride in what one is able to do; eager to invest self; eager to encounter new situations and new people
	Industry	To complete things	
	vs	vs	vs
	Inferiority	To make things together	Incompetent; inferior; inadequate; falling short of standards and expectations; unable to cope; afraid to venture forth; unwilling to try

Adapted from Erikson 1969, page 166

We have seen through the work of Erikson that children at every stage of their development have to negotiate certain life tasks of a psychological, physical, mental and social nature. The life tasks can be summarised as follows:

Summary of Erikson's life tasks

Life Stage	Life tasks – it is necessary to:
infancy 0–2 years	Develop attachment bonds to one or more individuals Know that objects and people still exist even when they are not visible Develop and test ideas through handling objects Develop movement and semi-coordinated skills
early childhood 2–4 years	Begin to develop self-control Begin to develop linguistic skills Explore and make believe play Develop further coordinated skills

Berne's Theory of Transactional Analysis

Berne's theory is included in this chapter because it is a useful working model of adult child relationship and will inform your work with children. The Theory of Transactional Analysis is a theory of personality. Although Freudian in origin, it explains personality development in simpler terms. Berne's analysis covers both personality development and interaction between people: Transactional Analysis (TA).

Eric Berne (1910–70), an American psychologist, provided a structural analysis of human feelings and human behaviour based on his clinical observations. Berne recognised that our patterns of behaviour are related to a system of feelings and experiences which operates on **three levels** or **ego states**. He defined ego states, now commonly referred to as mindsets, as a 'system of feelings which motivates a related set of behaviour patterns' (Berne, 1966). He named the ego states – **Child**, **Parent** and **Adult**, based on the three universals that all humans have in common:

▶ We all start life as **children**.
▶ We all have or had a **parent** figure who influenced us in the first three years of life.
▶ We all become **adult** eventually and are expected to make rational choices.

The basic concept of TA is that our experiences are recorded in the brain and nervous tissue. As individuals, we are all totally dependent upon our parent or parent figure. Therefore, all our experiences in the first few years of life are determined by our interaction with our parents or parent figure. It is memories of these experiences, and the feelings and reactions associated with them, that are never forgotten. These recordings are stored as though on video or audio tape. They can be replayed and our reactions recalled and even our feelings re-experienced.

The basic structure of personality is usually represented diagrammatically as three vertical touching circles, as shown below.

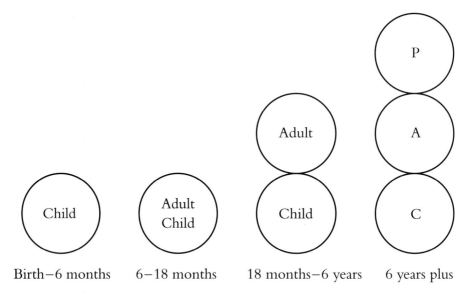

Chronological development of ego states

The three Bernian ego states

THE FIRST EGO STATE – CHILD

Child refers to the ego state or mindset evident in the emotional responses to the environment, characteristic of young infants.

Free child: We are born in a spontaneous state with no values or prejudices. We experience the first few months of life almost completely through our feelings; we feel happy and contented when we are fed, angry and frustrated when we are hungry. We react to life through our **Child ego state** as neither the Adult or Parent ego state is yet developed. This perception of the world through our feelings persists throughout our lives. The **Child** feelings of joy and anger recur. The **Free child** in us is obvious when we are mad, sad or glad. We are not allowed by our parent figure to remain in the free state for long because, our parents react to our egocentric behaviour. As we mature and develop, we learn to modify our behaviour to comply with the expectations of the parent figure. We learn to adapt (see page 43).

Adapted child: On the whole, we adapt unquestioningly to routines and rules of our parents although the Free child in us may resist. We learn to be polite and submissive and begin to have feelings such as guilt and anxiety. Examples of **Adapted child** behaviour are table manners and saying, 'sorry', 'please' and 'thank you'.

This adaptation or **Adapted child** behaviour begins to develop during the first year. The **Adapted child** can be positive or negative and can be further sub-divided into Compliant child or Rebellious child (see the table on page 124).

Compliant child: This is a consequence of over-protective parenting, where the growth of independence in children is stifled. Children learn to live up to the parent's or carer's expectations. They are reluctant to do things for themselves and appear confused and helpless.

Rebellious child: This results when rebellious, aggressive behaviour is inadvertently rewarded through the negative responses of the adult. Children learn that unsociable behaviour gains attention.

THE SECOND EGO STATE — ADULT

The **Adult** refers to the ego state or mindset that begins to develop separately from the Child (see above) at about eighteen months and is fully functioning by the age of eleven. The **Adult** is concerned with current reality, being objective and gathering information. The **Adult** is the rational, adaptable, intelligent part of our personality and functions by testing reality and estimating probabilities. When you are asking questions, giving answers, receiving or giving information, you are in your **Adult** mindset.

The **Adult** is the mediator of the personality, as behaviours from the Parent and Child are processed through the **Adult**.

THE THIRD EGO STATE — PARENT

As children, we adapt our behaviour to meet the expectations of our parents or parent figure. We also unconsciously absorb their values on right and wrong and how to help others. We learn a sense of responsibility by either wanting to help others or wanting to correct them. You often see the children in your care lecturing their peers on misdeeds or comforting and bandaging them up. Moral and political codes are absorbed into the **Parent** mindsets derived from parents and child carers. We are taught what to aim for, how we should shape our lives. From around the age of six years, the child begins to develop a separate **Parent** ego state (see the table on page 124).

There are two subdivisions of the Parent mindset:

Critical parent: This approach sets the rules and judges individuals by them. This is evident when an individual criticises others in a destructive way, e.g. 'You hopeless child'. Carers in their Critical parent mindset teach the child the 'do's' and 'don'ts' of behaviour. As a manager it is important to remember that children tend to do as we do and not necessarily as we say. The Adapted child stores up this information from the parent, and will carry it through into adult life.

Nurturing parent: This is the other side of the Parent, which expresses love and care and looks after people. All parents, consciously and unconsciously, pass on to their children precepts about what feelings and behaviours are acceptable within the family. The **Nurturing parent** offers support and protection. It is the manager who fulfils this role in the child care setting by helping staff, children and parents to resolve difficulties.

The table below shows you how the various parts in the Bernian personality interact. It is important for all the carers in the setting to recognise that communication with children operates on many levels: verbal and non-verbal. It will help you to picture clearly how group dynamics operate.

Verbal and non-verbal characteristics of ego states

	Critical parent	Nurturing parent	Adult	Free child	Adapted child compliant (C) rebellious (R)	
Words	Never Should Ought Do Don't	Let me Don't worry Be careful Well Done	Correct Where? Why? What?	Hi Fun Wow Great	Sorry Please Won't No	(C) (C) (R) (R)
Voice	Critical Condescending	Sympathetic Encouraging	Confident Enquiring	Excited Free	Apologetic Defiant	(C) (R)
Expressions	Frowning Pointing	Accepting Smiling	Thoughtful Interested	Spontaneous Uninhibited	Helpless Sullen	(C) (R)
Attitude	Judgmental Authoritarian	Understanding Caring	Open Evaluative	Curious Changeable	Agreeing Rebellious	(C) (R)

Children do not rationalise when they get their facts and values from only one source, namely the parent or caretaker figure. Children have to learn other points of view and other values. In most cases, this happens only when children physically leave their home environment to join a playgroup in somebody else's home or the library, church hall or nursery.

On a more general level therefore, as carer manager, you may wish to ask yourself: 'Does the child's behaviour in respect of their psychological, physical, mental and social development represent a retrograde step?' The child with a new baby in the family often resorts to attention-seeking behaviour: temper tantrums, thumb sucking or clinging on to their parent. The child feels displaced as the mother has to direct her attention to the needs of the new-born. Sibling rivalry develops.

'What are the results of the child's inappropriate behaviour?' The child may display such behaviour which, as a consequence, may impede the child's development. For example, they may be unable to play and enjoy social relationships with their peer group.

ACTIVITIES

After reading this chapter you may like to complete some of the following activities.

1. Draw up a profile of a child in your setting with behavioural problems that might be related to SEN.

2. Devise a plan for modifying the child's behaviour.

You may find it helpful to do the following:

▶ write up observations;
▶ think of an individual education plan;
▶ consider working with parents.

3. Read the following case study and discuss your understanding of TA with a colleague.

The following example shows how the three ego states interact.

You are short-staffed. You are exhausted after a long and intense day. You are about to lock up when a depressed mother arrives. As a manager the following thoughts (in the transactional framework) may be going through your head:

Parent: I ought to see her. She is distressed and it is my duty to listen to her difficulties, but she should have come earlier.

Adult: I understan d that she needs to talk, but I am extremely tired and will be unable to give her my full attention. I will see her briefly now and ask her to return at first break tomorrow.

Child: I am exhausted and I want to go home now! Why me!

Here, the **Adult** as mediator strikes a sensible balance between the **Parent** 'oughts' and the **Child** 'wants' to achieve a sensible compromise. Postponing the meeting satisfies both needs.

References

Berne, E. (1966) in Pitman, E. (1984) *Transactional Analysis for Social Workers and Counsellors*. London: Routledge.

DfEE (1994) *Code of Practice on the Identification and Assessment of Special Educational needs*. London: Central Office of Information, HMSO.

DfEE and SCAA (1996) *Nursery Education: Desirable Outcomes for Children's Learning*. Sudbury: DfEE Publications Centre.

Ilg, F. and Bates Ames, L. (1966) *The Gesell Institute's Child Behaviour*. New York: Harper & Row.

Further reading

Andreski, R. and Nicholls, S. (1997) 'Managing children's behaviour'. *Nursery World*, London.

Bettelheim, B. (1987) *A Good Enough Parent*. London: Thames and Hudson.

Paley, V. (1991) *The boy who would be a helicopter*. Cambridge, Mass.: Harvard University Press.

Miller, A. (1987) *The Drama of Being a Child*. London: Virago.

Rogers, C. (1961) *On Becoming a Person*. Boston: Houghton Miflin.

Tobin, J. et al (1989) *Pre-school in Three Cultures*. New Haven: Yale University Press.

7

Managing the Carers

Peter Drucker, credited with the idea of Management by Objectives, worked as a business adviser to a number of American corporations in the 1940s and 1950s. Drucker grouped into five categories what he saw as the process of management. In one of these categories, Developing People, Drucker sees the manager as the one who 'brings out what is in them or he stifles them. He strengthens their integrity or he corrupts them'. This chapter explores each of these five categories within the context of managing carers. Where appropriate, the categories are supported by related theories in the field.

Peter Drucker's management process

Drucker's five categories

1 Organising the Work — the tasks that have to be done, including staff recruitment
2 Setting Objectives — must determine what is the aim of the organisation
3 Motivating Employees — the ability to communicate information to enable staff to do their work
4 The Job of Measurement — the staff performance review set against agreed criteria
5 Developing People — one of the key roles the manager performs is that of helping staff to develop

Getting tasks done

Drucker believes that the work that needs to be done must be separated into manageable activities and manageable jobs. The jobs must be integrated into a formal organisation structure, and individuals must be chosen to fulfil the jobs. The way in which an organisation is structured can help or hinder its effectiveness and efficiency. Though this function of management (organising the work) may seem to have more relevance in a large commercial firm it is equally applicable to a small setting such as a nursery or playgroup. The number of staff, their skills and abilities, will determine how you facilitate the flow of work and the amount of delegation and supervision required. One of your responsibilities as carer manager is to interview, select and line manage staff. To do this you have to manage your time effectively. The aim is to invest your time for the greatest return. Drucker sees this as doing the right job: knowing what to do and when to do it – time management.

Organising time management

The management of time is the productive use of time and not just filling time. The latter is about being busy rather than working. The carer manager who is constantly interrupted through children demanding her attention will not be able to conduct an interview satisfactorily. The effective use of time is one element of time management, the other being efficiency: doing the right job in the correct manner. The interview mentioned above should be pre-planned and arrangements made for a private interview. The combination of effectiveness and efficiency is the key to the process of time management. To improve this aspect of management the carer manager needs to find the working style that best suits their personality. The most efficient methods depend upon identifying the work style and then matching it to the present task. There are six key efficiency techniques that can be used as a means of achieving the most productive return on time. They are shown in the table below.

A task efficiency audit

	Efficiency technique	Use of time
1	Find your best work style	Is the way you perform tasks consistent with your temperament? Do you respond well to change? Can you focus on a task for long periods or do you require frequent breaks?
2	Standardise	Wherever possible use proforma. It is important to find a common way to handle repetitive tasks.
3	Consolidate	Combine separate actions. In an informal session with carers you can cover a number of items.
4	Redistribute	Can you delegate? For example parents' induction into the setting could be assigned to a colleague.
5	Anticipate	Your planned activity requires special equipment. What advance preparation is required?
6	Fit means to an end	Prior to starting a complex activity it is useful to ask: can it be simplified? can it be reduced in detail?

Time saving devices

▶ **Answering machines** are a good investment for saving time as they control your telephone time. As the majority of in-coming calls will not be that urgent, resist the temptation to find out who is calling when you are otherwise occupied. Your highest priority should be based on your list of tasks for the day.

Answering machines are increasingly inexpensive and quite commonly found in most offices and homes. Make your message brief 'This is [your name and number] please leave your name and number and I'll return your call'. Lengthy responses are no longer necessary as answering machines are quite common-place and the majority of callers are familiar with the procedure.

▶ **Fax machines** are no longer the tools of large companies as the cost and above all the benefits of fax machines are making them more attractive to small organisations and householders. Depending on the model chosen, benefits include: immediate delivery of information; sending the same fax simultaneously to a wide circulation list; preset transmission to take advantage of cheap telephone rate times; combining the functions of telephone, fax, personal computer, printer and scanner in one unit.

▶ **Personal computers** (PCs) are inexpensive and extremely useful. They can be used for: proformas for standard letters, administrative documents (for example, financial planning sheets, records of staff salaries and cost sheets) children's records: you can create individual files to include records of assessment, individual play plans, medical records, child observations and activity sheets. Databases of details can be created for children, parents and external professional agencies and suppliers. Desktop publishing is useful for mounting displays.

▶ **Electronic mail** now called e-mail has become an important addition to most offices and homes. The electronic mailbox stores all the messages until it is convenient for you to access the mail, in the time you have allocated for this task. Your response to the mail will be determined by the importance and urgency you attach to the communication. E-mail is most convenient and relatively inexpensive. Cost is based on the volume of messages sent and received.

▶ **A photocopying machine** is a very useful time addition to most offices. In the child care setting it is possible to purchase a machine to suit the purpose intended and the money available. Although computers can generate, for example, copies of letters and activity sheets, a photocopying machine is quicker at generating the same paperwork and offers the added benefit of collation.

EXAMPLE

The carer manager, Justina, feels overwhelmed. There is little time during the day to prepare the team for the inspection visit that is eight months away. Her days are crowded with telephone calls, intrusions from suppliers, external agencies, parents, children and staff queries. The mail remains unopened. She takes account of her difficulties and decides to manage her time more effectively, in the following ways.

On a twelve month wall calendar she pencils in all the important dates: social service inspection, OFSTED visit, open evening, induction days, festivals, sports day, open days and supplier visits.

She calls a team meeting and assigns to each of the three members of staff an activity on the calendar. Their names are pencilled in as the lead person for that particular activity.

She acquires an answering machine and appoints a team member to filter her phone calls.

She assigns herself the period from 10.00 am to 11.00 am every day to update various record-keeping systems and record forward planning notes on the computer.

The filing system is organised to keep, for example, master copies of child assessment forms and staff rota.

Her own task list is updated on a daily basis so she can prioritise her personal workload.

Organising the recruitment of new staff

The task of selecting potential carers is important, as the management of any effective and efficient child care centre should have explicit standards for the setting and for the carers employed. Expected standards must comply with the Children Act 1989 or local authority guidelines, be known and explained to the carers.

When thinking of recruiting new staff it is important to consider carefully the nature of the vacant position from the point of view of 'Organising the work'. Doing the preparatory work of thinking through what the job entails (manageable activities and manageable jobs) will help you define the person specification for that position. You should think of:

- ▶ **Tasks** itemise the responsibilities for your new staff. Prioritise these responsibilities in descending order of importance.
- ▶ **Experience** will the job require past experience of working in a similar childcare environment?
- ▶ **Training** if the successful candidate requires further training will you have the time to give them 'in-service' training or the resources to afford external training?
- ▶ **Length of time** will you need a full-time carer or a sessional part-timer?
- ▶ **Authority** will the carer be allowed to deputise fully in your absence and have authority to make appointments for new parents to visit the provision?
- ▶ **Skills of the carer** do you require someone to work with a special group of children that need particular qualifications or personal qualities?

Another method of defining your needs is to draw up a job description. This should include:

- ▶ Job title
- ▶ Purpose of the job
- ▶ Main responsibilities
- ▶ General duties
- ▶ Person specification: desired achievements, qualifications and training, relevant past experience with children, job knowledge, aptitude and skills, personal qualities.

Job advertisement

Prospective candidates for the vacant position might be recruited from the following sources:

- ▶ through parents or members of your team;
- ▶ by recruiting from childcare courses at college;
- ▶ through advertising – local newspaper, journal, magazine;
- ▶ through local job centres or Training and Enterprise Council.

If you need to write an advertisement, emphasise the strengths of the provision: 'an opportunity for interesting and creative work'. You must be clear who you wish to attract for the position and the level of expertise you are seeking. Communicating standards to the carer is important and therefore these should be conveyed in the advertisement. All advertisements must comply with equal opportunities legislation (see Appendix 2).

Organising an interview

As a manager you will spend considerable time in face to face interactions with staff, parents, health professionals, education officials and others. The interview is a form of interaction that demands both organisation and a special technique.

Carer managers, as well as interviewing potential carers for jobs, may come across other types of interview:

Research interview

This type is used mainly to assess the effect of changes in practice or the organisation of services provided. For example, if the Under Eights Adviser wanted to evaluate induction programme provision in the borough they would seek your permission to conduct a research interview. From their findings, they could then judge how the programme might be monitored, improved, altered and what effects this might have on the children. The research interview can improve professional practice by highlighting areas of strengths and weaknesses.

Media interviews

This interview includes press, radio and television. The function of the media interview is to provide opinion, information and entertainment. If your local council proposed to close a playground popular with children in your care, the media might wish to interview you or members of your staff to ascertain what effects the closure would have on the children and your provision. Alternatively you might wish to initiate an interview with the media.

Appraisal interviews

Used extensively in industry, appraisal interviews are designed to evaluate staff performance and identify any staff development needs.

Selection interview

This is the commonest form of interviewing in child care. The main purpose of a selection interview is to choose the most suitable person for the job and for the candidate to choose your setting. Unlike a large organisation, in most child care settings it is unusual to have a panel of interviewers making the selection. In some settings it can be just the carer manager making the selection and the process can be an informal rather than a formal interview. Regardless of the process adopted, the criteria for selection should be based on:

▶ Is this the person suitable for the job?
▶ Will they be effective with the children?
▶ Will you enjoy working with them?
▶ Will they fit into your provision?

Handling different types of questions

As there are many forms of interviews, there are many different ways of asking questions. Biddle and Evenden (1980) identify six types:

CLOSED QUESTIONS

Usually require no more than a 'yes' or 'no' response. Best used:

▶ to obtain specific information;
▶ to open a conversation;
▶ to re-focus and clarify issues.

EXAMPLE

▶ to obtain specific information – Do you have a current First Aid certificate?
▶ to open a conversation – Are you comfortable?
▶ to re-focus and clarify issues – Are you willing to consider a temporary part-time position?

OPEN-ENDED QUESTIONS

These are the opposite to closed questions, demanding longer, descriptive answers. Best used:

▶ to explore ideas;
▶ to give the opportunity for a fuller response.

EXAMPLE

▶ to explore ideas – What do you think is the best way to help children new to the playgroup settle?
▶ opportunity for a fuller response – You mentioned in your CV that you have worked with children with special needs; what prompted you to pursue this?

Leading questions

Encourage the response which you wish to hear, or expect to hear and seldom gives any useful information as they emphasise your point of view.

EXAMPLE

▶ Some parents can be unsympathetic to minor injuries in their children. I imagine you wouldn't react in this way?

▶ I assume you know what is meant by the phrase 'Desirable Outcomes for Children's Learning'?

Probing questions

Seek more information about a subject you are currently discussing. Best used:

▶ to encourage the prospective candidate to build upon the information already given;

▶ to help the candidate make vague statements more precise;

▶ to elicit a clearer response;

▶ to give the candidate the opportunity to think about their initial response.

EXAMPLE

▶ I can see from your CV that you completed your NVQ in Child Care and Education while employed as a Nanny. How did you gather evidence for group activities?

Reflecting questions

This involves mirroring the candidate's response and is a way of confirming understanding. 'So you do work with children with special needs?'

EXAMPLE

▶ So you do believe that children should be given the opportunity to have their work displayed?
▶ You prefer childminding to your previous job then?

CONTROLLING QUESTIONS

Provide a way of directing, controlling and keeping the interview to time. When best used:

▶ to encourage the candidate to focus clearly on the question and not drift.
▶ to bring the candidate back to the point under discussion.

EXAMPLE

▶ Thank you for telling me about the provision of your setting. Can you tell me however the part you play in planning the curriculum?
▶ You have talked about the difficulties Abdhu has with English as a second language but how do you help him specifically?

Mapping for a formal selection interview

Interviews can be broken down into distinct stages:

▶ Pre-interview   Preparation
▶ The interview   Welcome
                    Acquiring information
                    Supplying information
                    Ending
▶ Post-interview   Reflecting
                    References

PRE-INTERVIEW – PREPARATION

It is usual for candidates to have either completed an application form or sent in a curriculum vitae (CV). From either of these documents you will be able to discover the carer's work history, education, training and interests. This information will establish whether the candidate meets your requirements (selection criteria) for the job as advertised and should be invited for an interview.

THE INTERVIEW

Welcome If possible, it is most welcoming for the candidate to have a tour of the setting. Introduce them to the children and observe their reactions. Most children respond immediately in a positive or negative way and you may want to weigh these reactions.

Acquiring information You will be in control of what is to happen and from your preparation you will have a series of questions (open and closed) to help you find out if this is the person you want. Ask specific rather than general questions.

EXAMPLE

'What would you do if, for example, I were away on a conference and you came in to find that children are arriving and two members of staff have telephoned to say they are ill?', rather than, 'How would you deal with a staff shortage?'

Supplying information At an appropriate point you should give an honest account of all the details of the job with reference to the job description. Your manner should make the candidate feel sufficiently comfortable to allow them to ask questions and reveal their personal qualities like humour, adaptability and curiosity.

POST-INTERVIEW

Reflecting You may have made notes during the interview and it's now time to collect your thoughts and think over the proceedings.

▶ Could you have handled the interview better?
▶ Did you achieve your goal? If not, why not?
▶ Does any one else need to know the result of the interview?

References These should be the prospective candidate's present or last employer, college tutor or head of sixth form. It is acceptable to adopt the informal approach and telephone the referee before sending out standard reference forms. You may learn more about the candidate's work methods through this informal chat with their referee.

Setting objectives

The setting of objectives must be done in relationship to each individual child. Through assessment of each child's progress you will, with your team, draw up curriculum plans for the long, medium and short term (Chapter 5). Objectives set for staff will therefore relate directly to the care and educational development targets for each child.

EXAMPLE

Three-year-old Abdul is not settled. It is his third week and he remains very insecure and withdrawn. He seems overwhelmed by the nursery environment. His stammer is more pronounced when he is asked a question directly by an adult and he struggles to find an answer. His vocabulary is limited to a few English words.

Objectives for Abdul's key worker

Short term
  - key worker to help him take a more active part in the setting and make him feel emotionally secure;
  - use topic web to display information from his country;
  - to assess his vocabulary;
  - to encourage him to associate with other children at the sand or water tray (standard practice for children who have emotional and/or language needs).

Medium term
  - to allow the speech therapist to advise on his stammer;
  - to get Abdul assistance from the second language coordinator;
  - to increase his participation in activities and encourage responsibility;
  - to begin to lessen time spent with key worker;
  - to assess his vocabulary.

Long term
  - to have full integration and participation;
  - to distance key worker before Abdul becomes over-dependent;
  - to assess his vocabulary.

Motivating and appraising staff

A team is best described as a group of people who share a common purpose in working together. Depending on the number of children in your setting, you may have a small team of four (i.e. three members and yourself) or you may have a much larger team. Irrespective of the size of the team, each individual in it needs to be effective for the team to be effective.

In Chapter 3 we noted that meeting children's needs can be understood using Maslow's theory. Similarly, drawing on the same motivational theory, you can identify the needs of the individual carer within your team. Charles Handy (1995) in *Understanding Organisations* draws our attention to the importance of motivation, by asking the question:

> *If we could understand, and could then predict, the ways in which individuals were motivated we could influence them by changing the components of that motivation process. Is that manipulation – or management?*

Motivation

Perhaps the easiest way to think of motivation is to regard it as the means whereby an individual performs an action because they wish to do so. Maslow's needs hierarchy assumes that individuals have a set of needs or desired outcomes.

Maslow's Theory of Motivation is arranged in a pyramid of five levels ranging from the essential survival needs at the base of the pyramid to self-fulfilment and personal growth at the apex (see page 50). According to Maslow, individuals work their way up the hierarchy. He believes that each level of need is dominant until adequately satisfied; only when the level becomes less important does the next level of need become a motivating factor. The exception to this is the need for self-actualisation which can never be satisfied.

Knowledge of the theory will help you promote effective team work as you can begin to define the needs of your team and, through manipulation or management, influence their behaviour.

Motivators include:

▶ Responsibility
▶ Recognition
▶ Achievement

▶ Task interest
▶ Advancement
▶ Growth.

Herzberg (1966) takes the view that these motivators (or satisfiers) create higher individual performance as they satisfy the individual's needs to achieve, learn and grow.

Though much criticised, the theory in application is useful as a diagnostic tool. For example, the carer who is constantly bothered about lack of supervision or poor pay is unlikely to become motivated. However if good hygiene factors (working conditions) prevail (see page 140), that weakens the source of dissatisfaction and leaves the way open for motivators to operate. The motivated carer needs a sense of achievement. Although sometimes it may be difficult to achieve in a small setting, the work should enable the carer to develop personally and professionally.

EXAMPLE

It was apparent to Justina, the carer manager, that after six months of working at the nursery Pam the new recruit seemed a little unfocused. Justina used the mid-year review appraisal to discuss this with Pam. All her observations were supported. Pam confessed to feeling somewhat de-motivated as her role was not as respected as the others in the team. The carer manager took the opportunity to give Pam a challenging task. She knew that Pam enjoyed community events and was very competent with the new desktop publishing software on the computer. A proposal was put to Pam: would she, with the help of parents, edit a monthly newsletter for the nursery? Pam had a chance to be creative and in charge of her own project. She also appreciated that it supported one of the manager's objectives for the nursery.

This objective was linked to one of the criteria of roles and responsibilities for effective learning to take place as set out by Cathy Nutbrown (1994).

▶ **Communicate with the nursery staff team, parent, children, other educators, other professionals.**

If the carer manager is able to involve everyone in the achievement of management objectives, this further helps to bolster an individual carer's self-esteem and motivation.

The job of measurement

Historically, the use of performance appraisal (PA) as a management tool comes from business organisations: Drucker's Management by Objectives (MBO). MBO is a process whereby senior managers and middle managers come together to establish objectives jointly: define areas of responsibility, identify common goals, agree performance indicators and targets. Each employee's actual performance can be appraised in relation to objectives set and comparisons made.

The rationale of this approach is to motivate staff through involving them in the setting of the objectives and thus promote their career development. An inherent part of the process, to improve the organisation's strategic planning, is the need for regular performance appraisal of staff by their line manager.

Motivating staff – a carer manager's checklist

Carer's needs	Manager's tasks
Self-Fulfilment concern with personal growth.	Foster creativity. Use training to advance their self-development. Help them set realistic goals.
Esteem requires opportunities to show competence.	Recognise expertise, value their contributions and acknowledge their strengths. Give opportunity to take responsibility within their area.
Belonging wants to be valued and considered as effective individual.	Provide induction programme for new staff. Be friendly and supportive. Make them feel included. Foster positive relationships. Keep them informed.
Safety psychological safety in job.	Refrain from using job security as a threat. Provide a comfortable environment.
Physiological basic requirements of food, warmth, shelter.	Provide for refreshments at coffee and tea time. Keep the setting at a comfortable ambient temperature.

Frederick Herzberg, in the 1950s, looked at what satisfied and motivated individuals in their work. In his book *Work and the nature of man*, Herzberg identified two sets of factors which he called **hygiene factors** and **motivator factors**.

Hygiene factors

Herzberg uses the term 'hygiene' to draw a direct parallel with medicine. If you consider that disease and infection can result in ill-health then similarly poor physical factors in the working environment can cause not medical ill-health but job dissatisfaction. Herzberg listed hygiene factors under the following four headings:

- ▶ **Physical Conditions:** the working environment, space, equipment, heating
- ▶ **Social Conditions:** friendliness of team and managers, shared breaks
- ▶ **Economic Conditions:** relates to pay, salary increases
- ▶ **Security Conditions:** job security, future prospects, training programmes

Herzberg believed that:

When people are dissatisfied with their work it is usually because of discontent with the environmental factors.

These factors have to be continually reviewed as satisfaction which depends upon environmental factors is not a lasting one.

MOTIVATOR FACTORS

Herzberg believes that motivation is an internal drive: it comes from the individual. Motivators stem from **job content** and not **job environment**. This is particularly evident in child care where salary and conditions often leave something to be desired.

In education, with the increase of league tables and the emphasis on raising standards, there is a shift toward MBO. As carer manager, you will need to evaluate your carers' performance and guide their career development plans. Therefore you will be involved with carrying out appraisal interviews and in some settings you yourself will be appraised by senior staff.

Why appraise?

If your carer is unaware of **what** they are supposed to be doing or **how** they are doing, their efforts could all be in vain. It is important for them to know what is required and how well they are performing. The appraisal interview is designed to help them improve their performance, work more effectively and efficiently and, as a result, be better prepared to fulfil their career potential. Appraisal must also be considered in a wider context as Penelope Leach (1994) states:

> *No amount of training enables a nursery worker to do better. If one baby is sucking the bottle on her lap when another wakes from a nap and a third drops a toy from a high chair, she cannot respond adequately to them all.*

In other words, before you rush to appraise the behaviour of the carer, **you must not forget to appraise both the task and material resources provided**.

SKILLS NEEDED

Appraisal is a two-way process between you and the carer. Appraisal interviewing is very different from selection interviewing (see page 132) because, especially in a small setting, the preparation needed for the interview and the interview itself is done in the context of an ongoing working relationship. The outcome of the appraisal interview could have long term effects on the working relationship. Appraisal is, therefore, a serious undertaking that requires good negotiating skills and it is advisable that managers seek some form of training prior to starting the process.

Appraisal Structure

Appraisal is essentially about giving your staff feedback on their work. The process will be more meaningful if you have an honest and open relationship. There are two key processes that will help you establish a more open relationship with your carer, they are: **feedback** and **self-disclosure**. Feedback can be a major force for good if it is honest, positive and constructive as feedback does have a significant impact on motivation. The more feedback the carer has on their performance, the better informed they will be as to how best to proceed.

There are many variations of the appraisal interview but whatever style is chosen, the following basic elements should be included.

▶ Beginning and establishing a rapport.
▶ Statement of purpose and structure.

Review

▶ Carer's self-evaluation, review of their performance.
▶ Your review of the carer's performance.

Future requirements

▶ Discussion on what is needed for the next appraisal meeting.
▶ Discussion on their career development plans.

Action plan

▶ Plan for their development: may require external training.

Developing people's potential

Staff development

Carers in the UK are generally better trained than their counterparts in Europe. In 18 British nurseries studied recently, only 20 per cent of their staff lacked formal training. The demands and pressure of the job are such that carers can be too depleted even to think about their child care and education performance situation let alone improve it. Therefore, it is imperative that as carer manager you seek ways to allow time for training and development. The Children Act 1989 supports this view:

> As working with young children is demanding and complex, care givers require a range of skills in order to provide good quality services. Training produces benefits for a variety of reasons. A trained person will understand how to respond sensitively to young children's needs . . . Training can make care givers more aware of stages in children's development and the need to adjust to the child's changing developmental needs. (Para. 6.4)

Training requirements

To meet the minimum requirements of the Children Act, you must ensure that:

▶ half of your staff possess a recognised child care qualification;
▶ one member should be a qualified first aider with a current qualification either from St John's Ambulance or the Red Cross;

▶ if food is served, one carer should be the holder of a Food Handling Certificate. The Food Handling Certificate is awarded by City & Guilds. Courses are held at most colleges of Further Education and some Adult Education Centres.

In-service training

As a carer manager an essential part of your responsibility is ongoing staff training. If you are unable to provide in-service training, then there are local networks that can offer a variety of short courses, seminars, talks, presentations and open college courses to cater for your specific needs. Training should include the following topics:

▶ 'Desirable Outcomes for Children's Learning'
▶ Equal Opportunities
▶ Partnership with Parents
▶ Child Protection
▶ HIV awareness
▶ Special Educational Needs
▶ Observation and Assessment
▶ Managing Children's behaviour.

National Vocational Qualifications (NVQs)

The National Council for Vocational Qualifications (NCVQ) and the Schools Curriculum and Assessment Authority (SCAA) have joined to form a new body as the Qualifications and Curriculum Authority (QCA). This new body is responsible for the curriculum and qualification from the under fives right through to Level 5 NVQs. In Early Years Care and Education the NVQs are designed to give carers an opportunity to obtain an award that is specifically relevant to their everyday work. There are two levels of the award in Early Years Care and Education; Level 2 and Level 3. The Level 2 award is suited to those carers who have a basic knowledge and experience of child care and education. Level 3 award is suited to those who have a supervisory role within a setting and thus extensive experience of child care.

The structure of the award reflects the desire by QCA to take into account individual needs. There are fixed units, mandatory units and option units that allow the candidate to select the units that best suit their needs. To achieve the full NVQ Early years Care and Education Level 2, the candidate must complete all eight mandatory units plus two units from the Options Group. The full Level 3 award requires the candidate to complete fourteen units: eleven mandatory plus three option units. A list of the awarding bodies is given on page 150.

Early Years Care and Education – Level 2 (10 units)

Mandatory Units – all 8 units must be chosen

C1	Support children's physical development needs
C4	Support children's social and emotional development
C8	Implement planned activities for sensory and intellectual development
C9	Implement planned activities for the development of language and communication skills
E1	Maintain an attractive, stimulating and reassuring environment for children
E2	Maintain the safety and security of children
M3	Contribute to the achievement of organisational requirements
P1	Relate to parents

Option Units – only 2 units must be chosen

C12	Feed babies
C13	Provide for babies' physical development needs
M1	Monitor, store and prepare materials and equipment
P9	Work with parents in a group
CU10	Contribute to the effectiveness of work teams

Early Years Care and Education – Level 3 (14 units)

Mandatory Units – all 11 units must be chosen

C2	Provide for children's physical needs
C3	Promote the physical development of children
C5	Promote children's social and emotional development
C7	Provide a framework for the management of behaviour
C10	Promote children's sensory and intellectual development
C11	Promote children's language and communication
C15	Contribute to the protection of children from abuse
C16	Observe and assess the behaviour and development of children
M7	Plan, implement and evaluate learning activities and experiences
P2	Establish and maintain relationships with parents
E3	Plan and equip environments for children

Option Units – only 3 units must be chosen

C14	Care for and promote the development of babies
C17	Promote the care and education of children with special needs
C18	Develop structured programmes for children with special needs
M6	Work with other professionals
M20	Inform and implement Management Committee policies and procedures
P4	Support parents in developing their parenting skills
P7	Visit and support a family in their own home
M2	Manage admissions, finance and operating systems in care and education settings
P5	Involve parents in group activities
P8	Establish and maintain a care and education service
C24	Support the development of children's literacy skills
C25	Support the development of children's mathematical skills
MC1/C1	Manage yourself
MC1/C4	Create effective working relationships

Communication

Communication in any group setting is an important activity. Communication of information, to assist the key processes of planning, coordination and control, is central to effective management. Carers may feel little sense of belonging where they are trusted with little information. There is the possibility that in the absence of effective communication carers may work without understanding, interest or motivation. It is important that carers are aware of what is expected of them. Effective communication can motivate them, give their jobs meaning and make personal development more likely as well as contribute to the smooth running and the ethos of the setting.

Communication can be verbal or non-verbal. The latter is communication without words and includes:

▶ Gestures
▶ Body posture
▶ Facial expression
▶ Tone, intonation
▶ Eye contact
▶ Physical proximity
▶ Appearance and dress

Non-verbal communication may be used deliberately instead of words: for example, crying, banging the door on leaving a room, kicking a chair, nodding in approval or pointing to something or someone. Research reveals that 93 per cent of an individual's communication is by non-verbal techniques.

An appreciation of non-verbal communication will help the receiver to modify or adjust their communication and response strategy as they will be better placed to 'read' situations.

Communication, to be effective, has to be a two-way process. A diagrammatic interpretation of the process of communication is as follows:

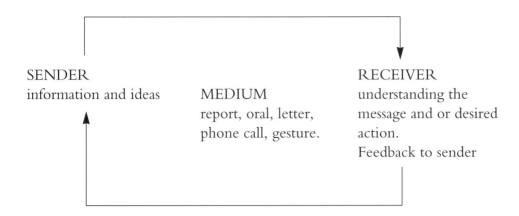

In any setting, the communication of information may take the form of:

- ▶ Giving directions, initiating action.
- ▶ Exchanging ideas.
- ▶ Giving or receiving information.
- ▶ Outlining plans or strategies.
- ▶ Formulating procedures or rules.
- ▶ Interviewing or reviewing staff.
- ▶ Completing work plans or job descriptions.
- ▶ Establishing and maintaining relationships.

THE NEED TO GIVE CLEAR COMMUNICATIONS

In child care, good communication is essential to advance the learning process, promote partnerships with parents, children and other professionals as well as getting any job completed. Problems can easily arise because of errors or weaknesses in the process of communication, for example:

- ▶ **Twisting or withholding of information by the sender**
- ▶ **Confusion due to lack of clarity or technical jargon**
- ▶ **Non-verbal signals contradicting the verbal message**
- ▶ **Overload – too much information to assimilate at any one time**
- ▶ **Cultural, educational, social differences between sender and receiver**
- ▶ **Selected hearing; hearing only what you wish to hear**

Barriers to communication

Barriers may arise from differences in ethnic, social or educational backgrounds, compounded by differences in age, gender and personality. There can be a failure to understand, listen and respond appropriately to the information. Where there are feelings of anxiety, fear or mistrust there is even a greater likelihood for misinterpretation.

Communication difficulties can be placed into three broad categories.

▶ misinterpretation about the actual content of the message;
▶ inter-personal problems causing a breakdown in communication;
▶ poor formal communication system.

EXAMPLES

Misinterpretation of the message
Maria has spent the first day as a Nanny looking after Jamil who is ill and running a temperature. Mother telephones to enquire after Jamil and says, 'If this keeps up can you give him a teaspoonful of Calpol? I'll be home in two hours.' Jamil wakes crying. Maria rushes to the kitchen and gives Jamil a tablespoon of the medicine. Here the carer misinterprets teaspoon for tablespoon. Inexperience and anxiety all compound the issue that results in the misinterpretation of the message.

Interpersonal problems
The childminder is having great difficulty understanding what Hiroki's mother says. 'You feed my child fish. No good.' The childminder is irritated by this comment and asks for an explanation. Hiroki's mother gathers up her son and leaves the house. The childminder immediately telephones the social services and asks for Hiroki to be removed from her care. She has had enough of the mother's abrupt and unappreciative attitude. A clash of culture sometimes may cause interpersonal difficulties; a breakdown in communication occurs because neither party is aware of the formalities or nuances of the other's culture.

Poor formal communication system
Prior to the open evening prospective parents are sent an induction pack for the nursery and an appointment time to meet with the carer manager. One parent telephones to cancel and reschedule her given appointment. The carer is full of apologies: she is unable to give any clear response as there is no indication as to where the diary for the open evening is kept and there is no information on the event. The formal

system in this example seems inefficient as the information cannot be accessed. Formal systems, to be useful, must be communicated to all staff.

A C T I V I T I E S

After reading this chapter you may like to complete some of the following activities.

1. WORK OUT A SCHEDULE OF QUESTIONS FOR A SELECTION INTERVIEW.
   ▶ Decide on the type of questions that you would use.
   ▶ Shape the questions to fit your setting.
   ▶ Where would you conduct the interview?

2. DRAW UP AN ADVERTISEMENT FOR A POST WITHIN YOUR SETTING.

Think about:

   ▶ Job description
   ▶ Person specification
   ▶ Strengths of your setting.

3. APPRAISE YOURSELF IN TERMS OF YOUR CAREER DEVELOPMENT.
   ▶ Does your current job fit into your overall career plan?
   ▶ Do you need further qualifications?
   ▶ What new areas would you like to explore?

4. CONSIDER MASLOW'S HIERARCHY OF NEEDS AND HERZBERG'S HYGIENE FACTORS
   ▶ In what ways are they similar?
   ▶ Which model best describes human motivation?
   ▶ Which is most applicable to child care?

5. WHAT ARE THE POTENTIAL BARRIERS TO COMMUNICATION IN YOUR SETTING?

6. USING THE TASK EFFICIENCY AUDIT ON PAGE 129, IDENTIFY AREAS WHERE YOUR PERFORMANCE CAN BE IMPROVED.

Useful Addresses

National Vocational Qualifications in Early Years Care and Education are awarded by the following awarding bodies:

Central Council for Education and Training in Social Work (CCETSW)
Derbyshire House
St. Chad's Street
London WC1H 8AD
Tel: 0171 239 9337

City and Guilds
1 Giltspur Street
London EC1A 9DD
Tel: 0171 294 2468

Council for Awards in Children's Care and Education (CACHE)
8 Chequer Street
St. Albans
Herts AL1 3XZ
Tel: 01727 847636

Edexcel
Stewart House
32 Russell Square
London WC1B 5DN
Tel: 0171 393 4444

Institute of Health and Care Development & Open University (IHCD/OU)
St. Bartholomews Court
18 Christmas Street
Bristol BS1 5BT
Tel: 0117 929 1029

Scottish Qualifications Authority (SQA)
Hanover House
24 Douglas Street
Glasgow G2 7NQ
Tel: 0141 248 7900

The awarding bodies can provide a list of the assessment centres that they have approved to run the award. Local libraries, Further Education Colleges, Adult centres, Training and Enterprise Councils (TECs) and the education department of Social Services can give information on how to access the awards in the immediate area.

Copies of the detailed occupational standards are available from:

Local Government Management Board
Layden House
76–86 Turnmill Street
London EC1M 5QU
Tel: 0171 296 660

References

Biddle, D. and Evenden, R. (1980) *Human Aspects of Management*. London: Institute of Personnel Management.

Druker, P. (1954) *The Practice of Management*. New York: Harper and Row.

Druker, P. (1973) *People and Performance*. New York: Harper.

Handy, C. (1995) *Understanding Organisations*. London: Penguin Books.

Herzberg, F. (1966) *Work and the Nature of Man*. Cleveland: World Publishing.

Leach, P. (1994) *Children First*. London: Penguin Books.

Nutbrown, C. (1994) *Threads of Thinking: Young Children Learning and the Role of Education*. London: Paul Chapman.

Further reading

Argyle, M. (1981) *The Psychology of Interpersonal Behaviour*. Harmondsworth: Penguin.

Alberdi de, L. (1990) *People Psychology and Business*. Cambridge: Cambridge University Press.

Barra, R. (1989) *Putting Quality Circles to Work*. New York: McGraw Hill.

Evans, D. (1986) *People, Communication and Organisations*. London: Pitman Publishing.

Hunt, J. (1981) *Managing People at Work*. London: Pan Books Ltd.

8

Managing Change

Much is written on how and why organisations resist change and much less about the process of change. Perhaps the former is easier to document because change as a concept is very elusive. Nonetheless change ought to be viewed as a process that needs to be managed rather than being permitted to 'occur'. Change can denote a deviation or a bold break. Change might also imply the imposition of a set of organisational aims and objectives that are a mismatch for what is actually happening. This chapter explores the meaning, planning and management of change.

The meaning of change

In the context of the organisation and management of the setting, change could relate to any of the following:

▶ **Changes in management and staff structure** A new manager will bring a different leadership style that will have an impact on carers, training, development and the ways of working with children, parents and professionals.

▶ **Changes in the environment** External influences, economic and social changes such as unemployment due to resiting of large industries, influx of asylum seekers, parental attitudes to pre-school provision can all bring about significant change within the setting.

▶ **Changes in technology** Technology can have an effect on the setting. For example, information technology is very much part of the learning environment and a tool for planning and organising schedules, rotas and work plans. The introduction of fax machines, photocopiers, the Internet and e-mail gives the manager greater access to a wider audience over a shorter period of time.

▶ **Changes in size of the setting** This might involve part closure or expansion due to mergers with neighbouring settings. The latter arrangement can provide greater economies of scale and saves on costs. The response to these changes results in organisation restructuring as either fewer or more carers have to be employed. The setting needs to maintain its efficiency in the face of change.

▶ **Changes in political influences**   The government can externally impose change through statutes, acts or other forms of legislation. For example, the Children Act 1989.

Each of the above can have a significant impact on the provision and may result in inevitable and rapid change to the internal environment.

Methods of change

Organisations can change by participative or authoritarian methods or modifications of either method.

PARTICIPATIVE METHOD

This is where staff are responsible for designing and carrying out the change; they are involved at every level. This method usually reflects a more constructive and productive approach to the process. For example, carers can engage in a SWOT analysis of strengths, weaknesses, opportunities and threats to plan the necessary changes in response to changes in the environment.

AUTHORITARIAN METHOD

Carers are given strict instructions and the line of command is usually through top-down announcements. Typically with this method, communication is rigidly controlled; in large organisations formal channels are used. You can use your legitimate power as carer manager to dictate change, but this approach may be counter-productive if the news is not well received by your carers.

The change itself may not always be viewed as desirable by those involved. Change is seldom viewed as the chance to rethink and reframe what goes on in a setting. It is seen more often as a problem and less as an opportunity. Nonetheless change has to be managed.

Theories and models of change

Process model for change

The Porras and Silvers (1991) Process Model looks at change for Organisational Development (OD) and Organisational Transformation (OT) situations. Much of what the psychologists discuss in their research is directed at large business organisations. The feature of their research relevant to child care is that for any change to result in a positive outcome, the new

aims and objectives needed for transformation must be translated into the
work setting before carers can begin to internalise this change.

A planned process model of change

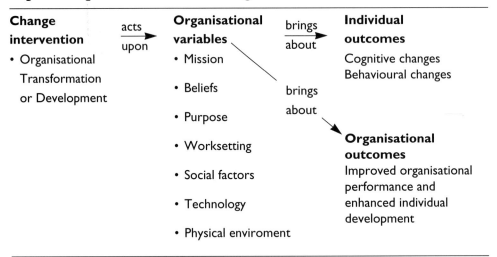

Change intervention	acts → upon	Organisational variables	brings about →	Individual outcomes

Change intervention
* Organisational Transformation or Development

acts → upon

Organisational variables
* Mission
* Beliefs
* Purpose
* Worksetting
* Social factors
* Technology
* Physical enviroment

brings about →

Individual outcomes
Cognitive changes
Behavioural changes

brings about ↘

Organisational outcomes
Improved organisational performance and enhanced individual development

Source: Sheila Hayward 1996 Applying Psychology to Organisations. London: Hodder & Stoughton

Force Field analysis

Kurt Lewin (1947) developed a model of change management that looks at
the micro perspective. As a carer manager, using Lewin's Force Field model
will require you to identify and systematically analyse those elements which
seek to assist change (**driving forces**) and those which oppose new methods
(**inhibitors**). The Force Field is the relative strengths between these
opposing forces and the equilibrium that arises from their opposition. For
example the 'Desirable Outcomes for Children's Learning', the inspection
process or new practices exerted by you as carer manager are driving forces.
Inhibitors to change will include inadequate training of staff, fear of the
unknown and preference for outdated practices.

Inhibitors to change

Carers as well as carer managers may resist change for a variety of reasons,
for example:

▶ Concerns regarding the validity of the proposed changes; i.e. change
  for change sake.
▶ Irrational feelings of fear and anxiety created by the proposed change.
▶ Feelings of inadequacy about having to retrain and perhaps be assessed
  on their ability to cope with changes.
▶ Feelings of anger at having changes imposed without due consultation.

▶ Feelings of being de-skilled by the introduction of new methods, practices or technology.

▶ Anxiety over the disruption to existing relations and work practices.

▶ Greater responsibility and loss of freedom.

DRIVING FORCES TO CHANGE

▶ The manner in which the change is suggested is inclusive.

▶ Expectations of personal gain.

▶ Stimulation to the mind and reduction of boredom.

▶ Source of the change is well respected.

▶ New and welcome challenge.

LEWIN'S MODEL OF CHANGE

Learning also involves re-learning – not merely learning something new but trying to unlearn what is already known.

Hunt (1996)

In essence this is the thinking behind Lewin's approach to changing human behaviour which suggests a three stage process to change work practices and overcome resistance: **unfreezing**, **changing** and **refreezing**.

Lewin's model of change

unfreeze	change	refreezing
existing behaviour	attitudes and behaviours	new behaviour

▶ **Unfreezing** Staff need a motive for changing their thinking, existing practices, values and behaviour. This is the most difficult stage of the process as it involves selling the change to staff. It can, however, be accelerated if the need for change is immediate, clear and associated with survival of the group or individual. The playgroup under threat of closure as fewer children attend will have to re-timetable staff or make some members redundant.

▶ **Changing** Once current practices are unfrozen, it is possible to work on the change process. It is important to recognise that change does not occur by itself. There has to be a source that drives the change. Staff need to relate to, and identify with, the new structures of desirable behaviours. Where appropriate, an education or training programme may be necessary to encourage carers to own the new changes. The implementation of the 'Desirable Outcomes for Children's Learning' requires carers to be involved in the staff development training essential for successful curriculum planning.

> **Refreezing** This is the third and last stage of the process. It involves reinforcement and consolidation to enable new skills, practices and behaviours to become firmly established. Behaviours need to be stabilised. A setting in a state of constant change would achieve very little. Your carers will need time for re-freezing to happen naturally.

Sources of resistance to change

Resisting change is seen by most psychologists as an attempt to maintain the status quo or the existing state of affairs. Sources of resistance to change may include some of the following:

Sources of resistance to change

Resistance	Source
Beliefs or attitudes	from a professional, cultural, religious or moral standing
Habits or past norms	a strong link to old methods will make it very difficult to get staff to relinquish practices
Group loyalty	groups tend to close ranks if their independent identity is under threat
Politics	if a power base is likely to be weakened

Overcoming resistance to change will largely depend on:

> **The pace of change** The more gradual the change, the easier it is for carers to plan and accommodate the proposed changes and unlearn redundant practices.
> **The breadth of change** Where total transformation is planned there will be greater feelings of anxiety and insecurity among your carers.
> **The manner of change** If there is a climate of fear or hostility associated with an introduction to the changes then carers will not be motivated positively to endorse the changes. The need for change must be made clear and where possible your carers should be actively participating in and identifying with the change. Therefore, the way in which the need for change is communicated is critical to the process.

The management of change

As a carer manager there are five steps you may take to implement change:

1 Determine the desire or need for change.
2 Have a clear definition of the operational changes that are necessary and

map out with your carers how the new ways of working will affect
children, carers and parents.

3 Analyse the possible reactions to the change by identifying the attitudes
and perspectives currently held by your carers and how these support their
present working practices.

4 Identify the attitudes and perspectives needed to enable carers to adapt
successfully to different working methods. Set up a pilot project.

5 Establish a timetable for change and action measures with your carers for
the purpose of modifying existing attitudes.

Culture and change

All settings will generate their own culture that will be made up of explicit
beliefs, underlying assumptions and values. Culture as a force for integration
and continuity has a far-reaching influence on the ways adults behave, react
and think in a setting. Culture, therefore, forms attitudes which are much
harder to change than behaviour. If there is a culture of trust, it will be far
easier to effect change. Staff will know that their concerns will be listened to
and difficulties recognised. More importantly, staff feedback on the
programme can be used to make adjustments. It is because of these aspects of
culture that it can be an important impetus to stimulate and manage change.

The three keys to successful change have been identified as:

▶ Participation
▶ Empathy
▶ Communication.

PARTICIPATION

In a small care setting this is easy to achieve as there are few layers of
management. If there is a culture of trust, then carers will be forthcoming
with ideas. To encourage participation, it is necessary to be clear when
your carers should be involved and how their participation will be made to
work.

EMPATHY

It is helpful to have an understanding of what change would mean for each
member of your staff. Empathy means putting yourself in the other person's
shoes. This personal interest in each member of your team will give you
considerable insight into what the likely difficulties with change might be
for each member.

COMMUNICATION

During the change process, effective communication is needed to create an understanding. The importance of communication and the barriers to successful communication are discussed in Chapter 7. However, those aspects of communication necessary to ease organisational changes within a setting and which are relevant to the change process are:

- ▶ Who needs to be informed about the change and who else wants to know?
- ▶ When should information be circulated about planned changes?
- ▶ How should the information be communicated? By telephone, letter, orally or in formal meeting?
- ▶ Feedback must be encouraged and obtained from all concerned. Questions need to be answered promptly and directly and all concerns, fears and anxieties should be allowed to be expressed.

All communication should be open and potential problems defined. As carer manager, you need to plan ahead. A proactive rather than reactive approach enables you to be less defensive. Many managers believe that withholding information increases their control but it also has the adverse effect of causing anxiety amongst staff. Your carers should be aware of the realistic goals and limits set, as this reduces anxiety and stress.

Managing stress in the carer

Stress occurs in any situation in which the individual perceives an external threat. When a threat is perceived the individual tries to cope with it and adapt, feelings of fear, anxiety or anger are generated.

(Lazarus and Folkman, 1984)

As a carer manager, you will encounter stress because you are responsible for the management of the health, welfare, and development of someone else's child during most of their waking hours. You will experience alongside your carers the following stress cycle that occurs in any social or work role:

1 **Anticipation** You will observe that the novice carer experiences significant stress prior to taking up her first post in anticipation of what the task of caring for a baby, toddler, or pre-school child might involve. The physical welfare of the child, and the emotional and intellectual demands of the post will all weigh heavily on the carer at this stage. While information and training can reduce stress it is important to remember that in the actual practical caring for a baby or child this training may be temporarily forgotten. This is why **support**, **practice** and **feedback** are

psychologically important for the carer under your supervision. Another source of stress is fear of the unknown: stereotypical assumptions about children can engender unwarranted anxiety since what is anticipated is seldom what happens.

2 **Honeymoon** The second stage is when the carer takes up the post and caring for the child is a novelty. The reality of care may be less stressful than anticipated because imagined fears have not been realised. However, the fear may be replaced by anxiety that the early enthusiasm for the job will not last. You may find that there are essential areas of practice that your carer is overlooking in their preference for those aspects of the post that they most enjoy.

3 **Plateau** There is a plateau in every job, during which the novelty wears off. In the early stages, the routines of changing, feeding, entertaining or instructing the child can appear tedious, because the carer cannot see beyond the routine. It is often during this stage that the child is left to their own devices while the carer busies him or herself with more administrative tasks. Gradually the carer will come to terms with the stress levels associated with caring for the child, accept the challenge of responsibility and contribute his or her own strengths to the care of the child.

4 **Termination** The day will come when the child moves on, for example, to full-time education or, in the case of childminder, to a group setting. Separation causes anxiety for the child. The carer may experience the same anxiety. She feels bereft at losing her surrogate-mother status and transferring the care of the child in whom she has invested much time and energy.

With children there are so many variables that it is sometimes very difficult to make definite plans for their future. For example, the state of health or developmental delay of a child can seriously alter one's projected plans; the intended school for which the child is registered may close or be unable to take the child; the carer's social circumstances may change. The carer must be prepared for change at every level and must always have alternative plans. Flexible planning will help the carer to cope with the variables associated with the developing child and diminish stress levels for both carer and child.

EXAMPLE

Three-year-old Zeeta, in India with her father for the past three weeks, was returning to the nursery in a fortnight. Zeeta had just lost her mother as the result of a long and painful illness and her key worker,

Janice, had tears in her eyes as she told the sad news to the children. She was very distressed. Janice knew she had to be brave but found it difficult. She rushed into the office. The carer manager, recognising Janice's stressed state quickly asked another carer to cover for Janice.

Subsequently, Janice arranged for all the children in the group to learn a song in Zeeta's home language to welcome Zeeta on her return. The key worker planned for Zeeta's aunt to come in daily to help the children learn the song. Janice was very anxious as she hoped this would comfort Zeeta.

It is quite normal for carers and parents to suffer stress according to expectations. In this example the carer manager needs to recognise, support and guide the carer through this painful experience and help the carer to help the children with this loss.

Managing stress in the child

Stress is a normal human experience and can be positive when it energises the carer to cope with a situation or challenge. In child care this will also involve managing the child's anxiety in stressful circumstances.

Likely causes of stress

If the carer has clearly fixed in her mind what is likely to cause stress at the different stages of the child's life and what is expected of her at each stage then negative stress can be greatly reduced. A sound knowledge of child development will make the carer more confident.

0–6 MONTHS

From **birth to four weeks**, the baby's main demand is physical comfort: being kept fed, dry, warm, held and soothed. He does not understand how he is pacified and cannot verbally ask for comfort.

From **six weeks**, he is beginning to strike at objects within his reach. By three months, he is putting everything into his mouth and turning, rolling and trying to push himself up. At this stage, children start to form a special relationship with their prime carer.

By **five months** he can sit up unassisted, enjoys dropping things, laughing and likes to play, sing and babble. Unfortunately, five months is also the time of the first tooth and the period of abrupt mood swings from crying to laughter. The stressed carer can manage the mutual tension at this stage with a lot of patience and making every event a learning experience. This is the time to be flexible and discard any fixed ideas about handling babies. It is important to overcome any anxiety by holding, cuddling, kissing and hugging him. Another strategy may be to vary his environment by going for a walk. Stress can also be dissipated by allowing the baby the company of other children whose company he enjoys.

Example

The childminder noted that five-month-old Tina was expecting her first tooth soon. Tina was very fretful and grizzly, constantly chewing her fists and dribbling excessively. Tina needed attention and comforting. Tina's bib had to be changed often as the dribbling and the mess from rusks were considerable. The childminder varied the afternoon programme and took the children to the activity centre. The new environment would help to distract Tina and help to minimise her fretfulness. There she could allow the others to play while she cuddled Tina and soothed her painful gums.

Teething can be a very distressing time for some infants. The carer with understanding of this developmental aspect is better equipped to cope with the child's behaviour and ease their stress.

6–12 months

From six months, he is extremely active, not only crawling but propelling himself across the floor. He will pull himself up onto furniture and try to climb stairs, This is a stressful time of standing alone then falling, walking, tumbling and trying to climb. The eight month old will be uttering his first words, naming and seeking help from his carers. The baby will have stranger anxiety and react tearfully to unknown faces.

The carer will have to be loving, energetic and understanding of the baby's need to explore at this age, without being overly concerned with cleanliness and order. The carer will need to keep a constant eye on him. This is the time to encourage him to cope with his environment as he begins to walk, talk and play.

EXAMPLE

Sam is nine months old. It is his fourth day at the parent and toddler group. Sam refuses to get down from his Nanny's lap. Sam sits on her lap while they play at the table with the face jigsaw. Harry approaches the table and Nanny encourages him to join in. Sam and Harry guided by Nanny complete the jigsaw. Sam is persuaded to join Harry to play with blocks on the floor. Sam plays happily until Harry's Granny comes over. Sam suddenly cries and rushes back to his Nanny. She hugs him reassuringly and tells him that it is alright.

The carer understands the child's stress and helps him to cope with a new environment and new faces. Here Sam displays stranger anxiety that produces his 'flight' response.

1–3 YEARS

From 12 months, the child begins to show a will of his own. He will oppose the will of the carer and cause trouble with older children. The behaviour

At two to three years old, children are beginning to assert and test themselves

may vary from doing nothing to refusing to play on their own. By two, he is becoming an individual, asserting himself and testing wills. At this stage, children are no longer obsessively interested in their prime carer. He becomes egocentric, asking constant questions. He wants to do things independently, like dressing and eating. He wants to run everywhere.

The carer at this stage must anticipate the child's stress in order to pre-empt their frustration. The carer has to encourage the child's curiosity and answer their many questions. The child wants to practise talking and needs to be spoken to in clear language, not just baby talk. Patience and imagination are required to read stories, provide new experiences and supervise planned outdoor activities. The carer must begin to foster social interaction amongst children because, contrary to Piaget's findings, it now seems clear that even very young children can de-centre and empathise with others.

EXAMPLE

Since the arrival of her baby brother Megan aged two and a half has exhibited attention seeking behaviour. Megan is clinging to her key worker Janice, is very aggressive to other children, throws temper tantrums and cries more often. She wraps her soft black and white cat Marbles in a blanket and carries it around like a baby. No one is allowed to play with Marbles. Megan reverts to sucking her thumb and wants to have her drinks from a bottle. Megan is not happy. Her carer recognises all the signs of sibling rivalry and understands Megan's feelings of displacement. Janice, with patience, comforts Megan through her tantrums and unreasonable behaviour. She reassures her that she is still very special. Janice, at story time, gives Megan a special place on her lap and asks Megan to tell the children about her new brother. What can he do?

Sibling rivalry can cause considerable stress, particularly to an only child. The unquestioned privilege of having the mother's attention is denied with the intrusion of a new baby. From the child's perspective the favoured position with the mother is severely under threat. The child feels emotionally abandoned, hence the regressive behaviour. The carer aware of the traumatic feelings caused by sibling rivalry can help the child overcome this displacement.

4–5 YEARS

From four, the child is struggling with being grown up yet longing to remain a baby at the same time. He will carry on long and involved conversations and yet will not like to be asked to repeat himself. Children at this age prefer groups of two or three companions. In the social context he may be very assertive and bossy. However, he is still vulnerable and may experience unreasonable fear of the dark for example. He cannot quite make a realistic distinction between truth and fable. The carer of the four year old has to provide comfort and support when nothing seems to be going right for him. At this age, he will not share his innermost feelings, therefore the carer needs to handle his anxieties with intuition. Children relax through listening to stories and playing games with a carer who enjoys their company. The carer has to be able to manage a balance for the child of outdoor play, indoor activities, television viewing and playing with friends.

EXAMPLE

Abdul was very excited by his first day at school. On his return he was unusually quiet. Nanny knew something was not quite right. Abdul gave short answers and seemed rather morose. It wasn't until bath time that she noticed Abdul's grazed shin. Abdul had been pushed in the playground by an older boy chasing a ball. Abdul, only four years and two months, began to sob. He related his tale and begged Nanny not to tell anyone.

She carefully dressed his shin as she listened attentively to his story. Abdul was distressed because he didn't make any friends and when he fell everyone laughed at him. He was also terrified of this boy whom he described: 'he was tall as a giant'. Nanny spent longer than usual putting Abdul to bed. She read him two bedtime stories, tucked him in with hugs and cuddles and held his hand until he fell asleep. There is a significant amount of stress involved in the transition from nursery to school. The carer mindful of this impact is able to recognise the difficulties that the child faces and act accordingly.

The carer aiming to control stress levels will be aware of what to expect at different ages, bearing in mind that each child's rate of development is specific. The greater the number of children to be cared for, the higher is the risk of stress. The carer must strive to share his or her time equitably to satisfy the needs of all the children. They must have the necessary skills to supervise activities and intervene where necessary in order to encourage the children to play together. Argumentative children will require sympathy and discussion in order to reduce their stress levels. It is important for the carer to keep her own stress levels under control.

The consequences of stress

The presence of stress within an individual can result in psychological and physical effects.

Psychological effects

Emotional problems: stress can cause personality changes making the individual tense, weepy, irritable, anxious or depressed.

Feelings of alienation from the work setting can damage relationships with others. The draining effect of inner emotional turmoil and conflict may lead to constant feelings of tension and fatigue. If stress is allowed to go unchecked, severe depression and other emotional problems are likely to develop and in turn cause stress-related illnesses.

Physical effects

Health problems: noticeable trembling, sweating, nausea, headaches, backache and difficulty in sleeping. Prolonged stress can lead to stomach ulcers, high blood pressure, weight loss and poor health in general. Excessive smoking, drinking and chocolate eating are now considered stress related behaviours that can lead to serious illnesses.

Behaviour problems: depending on the level and intensity of the stress, some individuals may display irrational and volatile behaviour while others may become oversensitive and withdraw into themselves. This withdrawal may be characterised by immature behaviour, a form of regression. Research shows that individuals under stress are more likely to have accidents caused by mistakes in judgement.

Loss of job satisfaction

As a carer manager you have a most responsible job that demands all your abilities. Too much stress can rob you of the energy that is very much needed when working with children. Too much stress makes you less effective at work and you will be unable to function to the best of your ability. It is important to recognise the warning signs of too much stress for both you and your carers.

Reducing stress

The following are a number of steps that you can take to reduce stress:

▶ Delegate to your staff as far as it is possible, ensuring that they can cope.

▶ Plan your time to maximise efficiency.
▶ Maintain a healthy perspective on life and work.
▶ Take sensible steps to reduce stress by having a regular programme of relaxation.
▶ Engage in some form of regular physical exercise.

Dealing with change in children's lives

You must be sensitive to the changing needs of the children in your care, and of those of their parents. Changes that can affect life both at home and at the care centre include:

A NEW BABY

The child can be prepared for the birth of their sibling. Playing with dolls can help the child to express their feelings. When the baby is born parents should be kept informed of any changes in the child's behaviour. Children can regress when a sibling is born.

EXAMPLE

Following the birth of a new baby, Rosie, aged four and the youngest in a family of three, showed regressive behaviour. She reverted to whining, a trait which carers had worked hard to modify six months earlier. Carers realised just how much the birth was affecting her through observing her play in the home corner. She played 'mummies and babies' to the exclusion of all other activities and alternated between crawling on the floor pretending to cry and 'giving birth' to dolls. Carers responded by turning the home corner into a baby clinic with the dual aims of extending Rosie's imaginative play and encouraging the other children to support Rosie in her play.

SIBLINGS AT THE CENTRE

There can be a few problems when children from the same family attend the setting. Separation from mother will be more difficult in the case of siblings, as both children may cling to the mother. The older child needs to be empowered to be responsible for introducing the younger child to toys and activities. Sibling rivalry may manifest itself in verbal disagreements or it may be physical for example: hitting. Sibling rivalry is stronger when the younger child is under 3 years of age. Fist fights are most common when one child is 2–3 years old and is prone to lash out with hands.

Methods you can employ to minimise conflict between siblings:

- ▶ ignore minor bickering;
- ▶ moderate as necessary in arguments;
- ▶ try to quell fighting which is out of control;
- ▶ keep siblings together when helping to resolve conflicts; separation only keeps the anger simmering;
- ▶ sit children on chairs and listen objectively to each side of the story;
- ▶ point out that though it is acceptable to disagree they must use words rather than hands to solve differences;
- ▶ summarise the problem for them;
- ▶ ask for possible solutions from the children;
- ▶ promote helpful suggestions;
- ▶ give praise when they manage to sort out arguments.

This method of dealing with conflict, provides children with a process for resolving rivalry.

An older child's anger can be directed in the following ways:

- ▶ pummel soft toys;
- ▶ thump clay and play-doh;
- ▶ boisterous play;
- ▶ knocking down towers made of bricks.

The younger child may need cuddles from carers and to be introduced to different and age appropriate activities.

Divorce

The child whose parents are going through a divorce will need reassurance that they are loved. The child's behaviour may be affected. As carer you must be particularly sensitive to the needs of a child experiencing divorce.

EXAMPLE

Denzil's parents are in the throes of an acrimonious divorce. Denzil, his mother and his older brother have moved in with the grandparents. Denzil is just about to turn three. He is very attached to his mother at the moment and throws tantrums when she does not come to collect him. Recently his tantrums have become more frequent and prolonged. Carers, recognising that he has emotionally regressed, spend time holding him until his tantrums subside. Staff, on the odd occasion, have had to take Denzil home.

Even though each child is different the following are typical reactions to divorce. The child may:

▶ become introverted, very withdrawn and sullen;
▶ become very dependent and cling to adults;
▶ have nightmares or sleep walk;
▶ cry for the absent parent;
▶ draw distorted people, scribble or move back a stage;
▶ use black excessively in paintings;
▶ use phrases like 'I hate you';
▶ become aggressive (e.g. refuse to go to bed);
▶ have feelings of guilt;
▶ have schemas of enclosure and enveloping.

SINGLE PARENTS

Some children may feel uncomfortable or embarrassed because they have one parent. You will need to be particularly sensitive when celebrating mother's or father's day.

CHANGES AT THE CENTRE

Change can be disruptive. When friends or carers are leaving, children should be prepared for these changes. They must be reassured that people do not simply disappear but they leave for a reason.

EXAMPLE

After three years Jo is leaving her job as Emma's Nanny to return to France. She has informed the parents of her decision. She plans to start preparing Emma, aged three, for the departure in four months' time. This warning of the leaving date well in advance gives the parents sufficient time to advertise and find someone suitable for Emma. Stories of children, adults and animals going away now become prominent on the bedtime reading list. Activities centre around post cards, post offices and travel agents.

After the departure, Emma wants an explanation from her parents as to why Jo has left her. To ease her sense of loss they repeat the story that Jo has told Emma several times in the past: she had to go back to a big school called a college now that her English has improved. Emma asks this question repeatedly of her parents and always they respond in the same way.

NEW CARER

The child will have to learn to trust a new adult. The child's routine may have to be altered.

EXAMPLE

The parents have interviewed and chosen a new nanny for Emma. Jo slowly begins the process of introducing Emma to her new carer. They meet on neutral ground in the park and go for a long walk. The relationship is fostered through several outings together before the new Nanny, Rose, is invited to the house for tea.

Emma gradually becomes familiar with Rose and is happy to spend a half day solely in her company. The carers meet to discuss the session and plan for Rose's arrival. The time Emma spends in Rose's company extends. Emma helps Jo to begin packing and helps to decide what she must take with her, like Paddington the bear. The acceptance of Rose and the separation from Jo is well underway. The final departure, though very sad, is less traumatic.

LEAVING FOR SCHOOL

Children will leave day-care to go to school. If there has been liaison with parents and school this transition should be smooth. Such liaison should include:

▶ transfer of shared records;
▶ reception teacher visits the setting;
▶ children and parents visit the school;

> ▶ reading books about starting school;
> ▶ carers talk about school to the children;
> ▶ school uniforms are placed in the dressing up box;
> ▶ encouraging role play (e.g. going to your new class on the first morning).

ACTIVITIES

After reading this chapter you may like to complete some of the following activities.

1. CALCULATE YOUR LIFE CHANGE SCORE.

Thomas Holmes and his colleagues (1967) developed a scale for measuring the seriousness of changes in American people's lives and related their score to their chances of becoming ill. Their theory was that stress had a direct effect on the body's immune system. The Survey of Recent Experiences (SRE) consists of 43 different life changes that have been scaled in Life Change Units (LCU) for the degree of adaptation they require. The work of Holmes and colleagues is now treated as seminal to any study on life stressors and although other researchers have changed some of the list, the principle remains the same. If appropriate, calculate your own LCU rating. If your score is more than 300 you should discuss the finding with a colleague or seek professional advice.

Holme's scale of stressful life changes

Rank	Life event	Mean value
1	Death of a spouse	100
2	Divorce	73
3	Marital separation	65
4	Jail term	63
5	Death of a close family member	63
6	Personal injury or illness	53
7	Marriage	50
8	Fired at work	47
9	Marital reconciliation	45
10	Retirement	45
11	Change in health of family member	44
12	Pregnancy	40
13	Sex difficulties	39
14	Gain of new family member	39
15	Business readjustment	38
16	Change in financial state	37

Rank	Life event	Mean value
17	Death of close friend	36
18	Change to different line of work	35
19	Change in number of arguments with spouse	35
20	Mortgage over $10,000	31
21	Foreclosure on mortgage loan	30
22	Change in responsibilities at work	29
23	Son or daughter leaving home	29
24	Trouble with in-laws	28
25	Outstanding personal achievement	26
26	Spouse begins or stops work	26
27	Begin or end school	26
28	Change in living conditions	25
29	Revision of personal habits	24
30	Trouble with boss	23
31	Change in hours or conditions	20
32	Change in residence	20
33	Change in schools	20
34	Change in recreation	19
35	Change in Church	19
36	Change in social activities	18
37	Mortgage or loan less than $10,000	17
38	Change in sleeping habits	16
39	Change in number of family get togethers	15
40	Change in eating habits	15
41	Vacation	13
42	Christmas	12
43	Minor violations with the law	11

2. WHY MIGHT STAFF RESIST CHANGE AND HOW CAN RESISTANCE BE MINIMISED?

You should consider:

▶ Inhibitors to change.
▶ Driving forces to change.
▶ Sources of resistance.

3. WHAT MEASURES WOULD YOU TAKE TO MANAGE STRESS IN A FOUR YEAR OLD?

You should consider:

▶ Setting a scenario.
▶ Identifying areas of stress.
▶ Outlining measures to minimise stress.

4. **WHAT HELP AND ADVICE WOULD YOU GIVE TO A COLLEAGUE SUFFERING STRESS AT WORK?**

You should consider the following areas:

▶ Lifestyle
▶ Professional advice
▶ Time management.

References

Hayward, S. (1996) *Applying Psychology to Organisations*. London: Hodder & Stoughton.

Lazarus, R. S. and Folkman, S. (1984) *Stress, Appraisal and Coping*. New York: Springer Publications.

Lewin, K. (1947) 'Group decision and social change' in Newcombe, T. and Hartley E. (eds) (1963) *Readings in Social Psychology*. New York: Holt, Reinhart and Winston.

Porras, J. and Silvers, R. C. (1991) 'Organisational Development and Transformation'. New York: *American Review of Psychology*, 42, 51–78.

Further reading

Miller, J. and Wiseman, S. (1986) *The Parent's Guide to Daycare*. London: Bantam.

Holmes, H. and Rahe, M. (1967) The social readjustment rating scale. *Journal of Psychosomatic Research* Vol. 11 213–218.

Velez, G. (1986) *The Parents Resource Book*. New York: New American Library.

Berger, K. (1995) *The Developing Person and the Process of Parenting: Childhood and Adolescence*. New York: Werth.

Freud, S. (1936) *The Problem of Anxiety*. New York: W. W. Norton.

Brooks, J. (1989) *The Process of Parenting*. London: Mayfield.

9

Managing the Inspection Process

Preparing for an inspection can be a time-consuming and stressful experience for managers and carers. This chapter will guide you through the inspection process from the initial registration as a provider to completion of your post-inspection Action Plan. Concrete suggestions and examples are given to help you manage the task.

Preparing for the inspection

Early years education policy

The government intends that immediately prior to statutory school entry (i.e. in the term following their fifth birthday), all children will receive three terms of free, part-time education. This is to be of a high standard and will be provided by all Local Education Authorities (LEAs) in partnership with the private and voluntary sectors. Providers must comply with the conditions and requirements of the Nursery Education and Grant-Maintained Schools Act 1996, which may be varied, waived, removed or added to at any time by the Secretary of State for Education and Employment.

Early Years Development Plans

- ▶ Every LEA in England has in place an Early Years Development Plan, approved by the Secretary of State for Education and Employment.
- ▶ These set out criteria for development and expansion of early years education in order to ensure free places for all four year olds.
- ▶ Under the Plan, grants will be paid to 'providers' educating four year olds in institutions defined below.

Grant eligibility

To receive a nursery grant, providers must be registered with the LEA. To be eligible for registration, a provider must fall into one of the following categories:

▶ A maintained school or grant maintained school.
▶ A local authority day nursery, family centre or combined centre providing day-care.
▶ An institution exempt from registration under the Children Act.
▶ An institution registered under section 71(1)(b) of the Children Act 1989, (pre-schools, playgroups, private day nurseries).
▶ An independent school finally registered with the DfEE.
▶ A provisionally registered independent school named or approved by a local authority or the Secretary of State in their statement of a child with special educational needs.
▶ Non-maintained special schools.
▶ A registered Portage Scheme.
▶ Childminders registered under section 71(1)(a) of the Children Act, subject to arrangements projected for September 1998.

THE ROLE OF THE LOCAL EDUCATION AUTHORITY

Each LEA must maintain a register of nursery education providers. The LEA will inform OFSTED when a non-maintained provider is added to their register. The provider can then be added to the central register and an inspection carried out at the earliest opportunity.

Registration as an eligible provider

Providers wishing to take part in their local Partnership (between LEAs, private and voluntary sectors) should contact their LEA in the first instance for an application form and a copy of the DfEE booklet *Guide for Providers Claiming Nursery Education Grant*.

Once centres have been accepted for inspection, they will receive:

▶ a covering letter;
▶ claim forms;
▶ the booklet *Nursery Education: Desirable Outcomes for Children's Learning*;
▶ a Self-Appraisal Schedule.

CONDITIONS FOR REGISTRATION

Providers must agree to:

▶ Work towards SCAA's six 'Desirable Outcomes' to be found in the publication *Nursery Education: Desirable Outcomes for Children's Learning on Entering Compulsory Education*.
▶ Teach English as part of the educational programme where it is not the main language of communication in the setting.

▶ Offer at least one session of two and one half hours per week for at least 33 weeks over the three terms for which the child is eligible for grant. Where more sessions are offered, these must average two and one half hours each over one week.

▶ In keeping with the Children Act 1989, apply adult:child ratios for 3–5 year olds of 1:8, 1:10 or 1:13, depending on staff qualifications and timetables.

▶ Assess the suitability of staff to work with young children in accordance with the Home Office booklet *Safe from Harm*.

▶ Satisfy a Registered Nursery Education Inspector (RgNI) that the educational programme is of an acceptable standard.

THE SELF-APPRAISAL SCHEDULE

The purpose of this form is to enable you to assess if your setting is ready for inspection. It is one of the documents which must be sent to the Inspector before the inspection visit. It is to be completed after discussion meetings involving the whole staff to evaluate your provision in the following areas of focus for the inspection:

▶ **Staff:** numbers, adult:child ratio, roles and responsibilities, qualifications and experience, plans for training and development, assessment, shared aims and objectives.

▶ **Education programme:** areas of strength and areas for development with respect to curriculum, provision and planning, leading to the attainment of all the 'Desirable Outcomes for Children's Learning on Entering Compulsory Education'; assessment of your programme.

▶ **Assessment and recording** of children's achievements in their progress towards the six 'Desirable Outcomes'.

▶ **Organisation of sessions:** to take account of the understanding, interests, involvement and concentration of four year olds; to enable them to work independently and in groups with different adults; to ensure that they can make full use of available space and a graded range of materials and equipment.

▶ **Premises and equipment:** should be adequate and consistent with work towards the whole range of 'Desirable Outcomes', with indoor and outdoor provision.

▶ **Children's welfare:** with special emphasis on policies for special needs (including working with other professionals), behaviour, equal opportunities, and operation of local authority child protection procedures.

▶ **Partnership with parents:** parents should be informed, involved in their children's learning and share progress reports.

▶ **Quality assurance:** internal and external reviews of provision and staff, action plans.

Published information for parents

Providers who receive a nursery grant must make available to parents of eligible children the following information about the setting:

▶ Details of the premises and equipment.
▶ Staff numbers, qualifications, training, ratio of adults to children.
▶ Educational programme and activities.
▶ Policy and provision for children with special educational needs (with regard to the 'SEN Code of Practice' and 'Guidance on the application of the Code to institutions outside the maintained sector of education who wish to redeem nursery education vouchers').
▶ The policies regarding: health and safety, discipline, equal opportunities, complaints.
▶ Admissions policy and procedure.
▶ Term dates and timetable.
▶ Fees.
▶ Procedure for recording and reporting children's progress.

In addition, you must provide a copy of your most recent nursery education inspection report and resulting action plan.

Preparing for the inspection visit

As manager, you will be contacted by the Inspecting Contractor for your setting, who will appoint an Inspector and send you an information pack containing the following:

▶ a Notice to Parents which you are required to display;
▶ a Setting Confirmation Form to complete and return;
▶ a **Manager's Form**.

The latter asks for details about your setting needed by the Inspector for entry in the first part of their Inspection Report. It must be completed promptly and returned to the Inspector prior to the inspection itself.

In addition to the Manager's Form, you should send the Inspector the following information before the inspection:

▶ published information for parents including details of staffing, admission arrangements, educational programme;
▶ your policy and provision for children with special educational needs;
▶ any other relevant policy documents;

▶ your completed Self-Appraisal Form;
▶ the programme or timetable of work that you will be doing during the week of the inspection and, in particular, during the time of the inspection visit.

The booklet *Are you ready for your inspection?* provided by OFSTED sets out the inspection process clearly and should be familiar to all staff.

Preparing your educational provision for inspection

Long, medium and short-term planning are discussed in detail in Chapter 5. For the purposes of preparing your educational provision for inspection, the following example offers planning around the cross-curricular topic of 'Growing' which spans the six 'Desirable Outcomes' and addresses many of the learning aspects within each area. The plan below shows the results of a staff 'brainstorming' session and links their ideas to the 'Desirable Outcomes'.

Growing

PERSONAL AND SOCIAL DEVELOPMENT

▶ Children establish effective working relationships with other children and with adults during the course of this topic because it relies upon cooperation.
▶ Children work as part of a group to make measurements of themselves, gaining self-respect, and seek help where needed.
▶ They explore new aspects of themselves (i.e. height and weight)
▶ They solve simple practical problems of how to record growth of children and plants.
▶ They treat plants and animals with care and concern and take turns using the bug box and the magnifying glass.
▶ They demonstrate independence in personal hygiene as they wash their hands after handling pond water.
▶ They show wonder in response to their experiences of the natural world.
▶ They concentrate and persevere in their learning using reference books, friezes and magnifiers.

LANGUAGE AND LITERATURE

▶ In large groups, children listen attentively to information about frogs.
▶ In small groups, children talk about their experiences of babies.
▶ They add new words to their vocabulary: frog spawn, tadpole, bulb, tulip, daffodil.
▶ They listen and respond to stories: *Avocado Baby*, *The Bear's Water Picnic*; and poems: 'When We Were Very Young'.

▶ They invent their own stories and participate in role play based on families.

▶ They use reference books intelligently, handling them carefully.

▶ They associate sounds with patterns in rhymes: 'Five fat peas in a pea pod pressed'.

▶ They recognise their own names on labels for the growth chart.

▶ They draw pictures of babies and other family members and name them, often using symbols, letters or writing.

▶ They write their own names on cut-outs of their hands and feet.

MATHEMATICS

▶ Children use mathematical language such as: 'bigger than, tall, short, long, more than' to describe size and quantity.

▶ They recognise patterns of growth; e.g. from egg to tadpole to frog, and represent these in drawings.

▶ They are familiar with number rhymes: 'I have two eyes to see with', songs: 'Five little speckled frogs' and demonstrate awareness of number operations.

▶ They compare, sort and sequence cut-outs of their hands and feet.

▶ They count tadpoles in the bug box.

▶ They recognise numbers to 10 and use them in counting tadpoles and family members.

▶ They record larger numbers in growth charts of amaryllis and daffodils.

▶ They use a growth chart to record their heights and scales to measure their weights.

▶ They make a bar chart to compare their weights.

KNOWLEDGE AND UNDERSTANDING OF THE WORLD

▶ Children talk about their bodies, comparing similarities and differences in size, weight, hair and eye colour.

▶ They talk about their families past and present and recall and recount events from when they were younger, noting how they have changed and 'grown up'.

▶ They look in detail at daffodils and narcissus, noting similarities and differences.

▶ They observe frog spawn, tadpoles and frogs closely, looking at patterns and change.

▶ They use a frieze on the life cycle of the frog to understand how and why development takes place.

▶ They use the bug box and magnifying glass to observe tadpoles.

▶ Using a tape recorder, they record their singing and instrument playing.

PHYSICAL DEVELOPMENT

▶ Children move confidently and imaginatively to music and mime actions of tadpoles and frogs.

▶ They do stretching exercises to imitate growth in plants and show awareness of space and others.

▶ They exercise to 'Head, shoulders, knees and toes', demonstrating control and coordination.

▶ They dig in the garden, handling appropriate tools to plant bulbs and seeds.

▶ They walk to the park to gather frog spawn from the pond.

CREATIVE DEVELOPMENT

▶ Children explore colour and demonstrate their powers of observation by mixing paints to match blooms of daffodils, narcissus and amaryllis.

▶ They use the paints that they mixed in their paintings.

▶ They use their imagination in acting out 'when we were babies' role play.

▶ They model frogs from clay in three dimensions and paint them 'frog' colour with spots.

▶ They show their increasing ability to listen by imitating the sound of frogs' croaking which they heard on a tape.

▶ They sing 'Five little speckled frogs'.

▶ They use their imagination and communicate their feelings by playing musical instruments.

The inspection

The inspection visit

Once a date has been agreed for the inspection, the Inspector will contact you to make arrangements for the inspection visit. These will include an explanation of how the inspection will be conducted, identification of staff members with whom the Inspector may wish to have discussions, and agreement with you about when and where any such discussions should best take place in order to minimise disruption. The Inspector will also wish to agree how and where the oral feedback at the end of the inspection is to be given and who should be present. During the visit, which will normally last one day or two half days, the Inspector will expect to see certain information or documentary evidence such as:

▶ Samples of curriculum planning sheets or timetables indicating what activities children will do and what areas of learning staff intend to cover.

▶ Examples of children's work.
▶ Education plans for individual children, especially those with special educational needs.
▶ Assessments of children, especially upon entry or when leaving the setting.
▶ Records of children's progress.
▶ Reports shared with parents.
▶ Registers of attendance.
▶ Any other written evidence that you wish to be taken into consideration.

The Inspector will be looking for a balanced programme which contributes to children's progress in all six areas (see page 89) of learning. It is accepted, however, that during the inspection it may not be possible for the Inspector to observe direct or indirect teaching in some areas of learning. If this is the case, you will need to provide other evidence of children's learning. This might come from curriculum plans, records of children's progress or photographs, videos, samples and displays of children's previous activities and work. Where no such evidence is available, the Inspector will have to report weaknesses in your programme.

Inspection of the educational provision

The purpose of the inspection is to identify strengths and weaknesses of educational provision so that providers can improve the quality of education they offer. In this way they help children, by the age of five, to achieve the Desirable Outcomes defined by SCAA. (OFSTED)

The Inspector is required to report on four aspects of your educational provision:

1 The planning and content of the educational programme

The Inspector will be evaluating the planning and content of your educational programme and its contribution to children's attainment and progress in the six areas of learning. You will need to show the Inspector effective, written plans which are shared with parents and identify what children will be learning.

Long-term curriculum planning should ensure that all six areas are covered in a broad, balanced and coherent way. You should also aim to address all the learning aspects within each area. The Inspector will be looking for satisfactory provision in language and literacy and mathematics and will expect to see some activities specifically linked to these areas.

There should be evidence of continuity and progression in your programme. It should build systematically on what children know and can do then move them on steadily to new knowledge and skills, aiming towards the expectations for children's learning at compulsory school age.

Medium-term planning of activities should fit into the context of your longer-term plans and will therefore, also be clearly linked to the 'Desirable Outcomes'. The Inspector will look at your plans containing details about:

▶ what children will be doing and learning during the inspection visit;
▶ how they will be arranged in small and large groups;
▶ which members of staff will be assigned to specific activities.

Using the results of regular assessments of children's progress to inform planning will ensure that your programme reflects the age/stage development of all children. If there are any children with special educational needs, for whom English is an additional language, or who are more able, you must be able to satisfy the Inspector that you have adapted activities to allow these children equality of access and the opportunity to progress towards the 'Desirable Outcomes' at their own pace.

2 The quality of teaching

The Inspector will wish to verify that staff have knowledge and understanding of the six areas of learning. This judgement will be based on how your teaching plans reflect the 'Desirable Outcomes' and to what extent the teaching achieves your planned learning objectives. The Inspector will arrive at this judgement through observation of teaching and discussion with staff. The training and experience of staff will also be taken into consideration.

The Inspector will need affirmation that staff have appropriate expectations for children's progress and attainment based on their own knowledge of the six areas of learning, their experience of children's past achievements and their aims for moving children on, taking into account children's age and stage of learning. This will be evident in the group's short-term plans.

Judgements will also be made about how effectively your short-term planning is implemented in order to develop children's knowledge, understanding and skills in all six areas of learning.

Your choice of teaching methods should be determined by:

▶ the learning objectives of the session;
▶ the numbers of children;
▶ what children have already learned;
▶ the resources available;
▶ the accommodation available in your setting;
▶ effectiveness of teaching methods in promoting the 'Desirable Outcomes'.

Staff-child interaction is essential. Staff should:

▶ spend much of their time working directly with children;
▶ give clear explanations;
▶ use effective methods of questioning;
▶ encourage children to think and become independent;
▶ intervene to direct and support children to develop and consolidate their learning.

Inspectors will also look at how staff group children for activities. There must be opportunities for children to work individually and in small and large groups depending on the type of activity and the planned learning objectives. There must also be a balance between teacher directed, purposeful, or structured activities and child initiated or chosen activities.

If there are children in your setting who have special educational needs, who are advanced for their age or who speak English as an additional language, you will have to satisfy the Inspector that you and your staff have adapted activities to meet the particular needs of these children.

Your teaching should provide:

▶ First hand experiences.
▶ A mix of activities involving practical activity and problem solving to extend children's knowledge and understanding and develop their skills.
▶ Opportunities for purposeful play, talk and direct enquiry.
▶ The best possible use of space, materials and equipment, to give children a broad, stimulating and interesting programme.
▶ Good use of the resources available.
▶ Best deployment of staff and other adults.

As manager, you will be interviewed by the Inspector for about half an hour about how you and your staff work together to plan a balanced programme for all children (including those who attend for fewer than five sessions), and how you use the strengths and skills of your staff. You will also need to discuss your system for assessing children's progress and sharing this with parents. Involvement of parents in your programme may also be discussed. The inspector will ask about your methods for evaluating teaching in the setting and about in-service training for staff. Your staff may be asked why they are doing a piece of work and why they have chosen to carry it out in a certain way.

3 *The ways in which children's attainment and progress are assessed*

The Inspector will make judgements about your group's methods for assessing children's attainment and progress towards the 'Desirable Outcomes'. The Inspector will be looking for a system of regular and ongoing observation of all children. These observations should be recorded and should form the basis for assessing children's progress. Judgements will also be made as to how this assessment information is used in planning in order to provide children with a suitable educational programme.

4 *The effectiveness of partnership with parents and carers*

The Inspector will make judgements about how you make available to parents essential information about your provision. Judgements will also be made on your methods for informing parents about their children's attainment and progress. You should be able to demonstrate ways in which parents are involved in their children's learning and are made welcome in the setting.

The inspection report

After the inspection, the Inspector will write a formal report which you will receive within three weeks of the visit. You are responsible for making the report available to parents of children with Nursery Education Grants. The report will contain:

1 **The main findings**   These include a statement of the strengths and

weaknesses of the educational provision and its contribution to the 'Desirable Outcomes for Children's Learning'; a summary of the judgements about whether the educational provision will promote the 'Desirable Outcomes'; a recommendation as to whether or not the setting

Making progress towards the 'Desirable Outcomes': knowledge and understanding of the world

should be validated and on the timing for the next inspection. Judgements are also made on the planning of the educational programme, the quality of teaching and assessment and partnership with parents and carers.

2 **Key issues for action**   The report must also include a list of areas in which you should make progress in order to improve the quality and standards of the educational provision.

The action plan

Within 40 days of receiving the inspection report, you are required to draw up an action plan, indicating how you and your staff intend to address the key issues for action in order to improve your educational practice within the next 12 months. Reference to your Self-Appraisal Schedule, which acts as a baseline assessment of your setting, will help you to measure the progress made since your decision to become a provider. The inspection report will give you guidance for future improvements. The DfEE publication entitled *Action plans: A Guide for Private, Voluntary and Independent Providers of Nursery Education* contains valuable advice and examples of action plans.

Given the above guidelines, it is your responsibility to meet with your staff to draw up an action plan specific to your setting.

ACTIVITIES

1. COMPLETE A SELF-APPRAISAL SCHEDULE FOR YOUR SETTING. THIS IS AVAILABLE FROM THE DfEE (SEE REFERENCES BELOW).

2. PLAN A LEARNING PROGRAMME FOR THE MONTH DURING WHICH AN INSPECTION WILL TAKE PLACE. CONSIDER:

▶ a topic or theme which reflects children's current interests;
▶ what materials and resources you will need;
▶ how individual children's needs will be met by the programme.

3. ASSEMBLE DOCUMENTARY EVIDENCE OF LEARNING THAT HAS TAKEN PLACE OVER ONE HALF TERM. THIS MIGHT INCLUDE:

▶ planning documents;
▶ examples of children's work;
▶ photographs and videos;
▶ records of individual children's progress.

Useful addresses

DfEE Publications Centre
PO Box 5050
Sudbury
Suffolk CO10 6ZQ
Tel: 0845 602 2260
Fax: 0845 603 3360

OFSTED
Alexandra House
29–33 Kingsway
London WC2B 6SE
Tel 0171 421 6800

References

DfEE and SCAA (1996) *Nursery Education: Desirable Outcomes for Children's Learning.* Sudbury: DfEE Publications Centre.

Code of Practice on the Identification and Assessment of Special Educational Needs. Ibid., 1994

Guidance on the application of the Code to institutions outside the maintained sector of education who wish to redeem nursery education vouchers. Ibid., 1996

Guide for Providers Claiming Nursery Education Grant. Ibid., 1997

Action Plans. Ibid., 1997

Early Years Development Partnership and Plans: Guidance. Ibid., 1997

Self-Appraisal Schedule. Ibid., February 1998

Early Years Development Partnership and Plans: Requirements of Grant. Ibid., 1998

Are You Ready For Your Inspection? London: Office for Standards in Education

Burningham, J. (1982) *Avocado Baby.* London: Picture Lions.

Milne, A. A. (1989) *When We Were Very Young.* London: Methuen.

Smith, D. R. (1993) *Safe from Harm: Code of Practice for Safeguarding the Welfare of Children in Voluntary Organisations in England and Wales.* London: Home Office.

Yeoman, J. and Blake, Q. (1970) *The Bear's Water Picnic.* London: Macmillan.

10

Managing Children's Health and Welfare

This chapter looks at draft policies for ensuring children's health, safety and welfare in the child care setting. Any provider's policy must be specific to the provision and should be drawn up with carers and community members working in collaboration. The draft policies provide a working model for policy formulation. At the core of every policy must be the welfare of the child. Child carers are required by the Children Act 1989 to have regard for legal aspects of child care provision. Included in this chapter are some legal guidelines for good practice based on relevant legislation.

Health and hygiene policy

It is imperative if children are to benefit from the educational programme that high standards are maintained within the setting to promote a healthy environment. These standards are as follows:

- Food is stored at the correct temperature and snacks are prepared hygienically.
- Hands are washed before handling food.
- Hands are washed after using the toilet.
- Paper towels are used for drying hands.
- Disposable gloves are worn when dealing with body fluids; blood, urine.
- A dilute solution of bleach (1:10) is used when cleaning up spillage.
- Tissues are available for children to use.
- Children are encouraged to cover their mouths when coughing.
- Cuts and open sores must be covered with plasters.
- Parents are asked to keep their children at home if they are feeling unwell or have any infection.
- Parents must find out from their GP when the child can safely be allowed to return to the setting.
- The manager must be notified as to the nature of the illness as soon as possible in order to be able to alert other parents, and observe carefully any child who appears unwell.

▶ Children who are sent home with vomiting or diarrhoea must remain at home until at least 24 hours have elapsed since the last attack.

▶ Parents provide written authorisation for carers to administer medications to children.

Immunisation

In the UK parents can choose whether or not to have their children immunised. Immunisation only works if most children are vaccinated. If many parents take the decision not to have their children vaccinated then there is the likelihood of infectious diseases spreading. This particularly applies to child care settings where large numbers of children congregated together increase the risk of infection being transmitted from child to child. Although immunisation is the safest form of protection against infectious diseases some children may suffer adverse reactions: fevers, fits and in extreme cases brain damage.

MENINGITIS

One of the most serious childhood illnesses is **Meningitis**. This is an inflammation of the lining of the brain which can be caused by several types of bacteria or virus. The **Hib vaccine** protects against the bacterial infection called Haemophilus influenzae type b.

Hib is an infection that can cause a number of serious illnesses including:

▶ Blood poisoning (septicaemia)
▶ Pneumonia
▶ Severe swelling in the throat
▶ Meningitis.

Since the introduction of the Hib vaccine in 1992 the number of children with Hib meningitis has dropped by 95 per cent. As there are no homeopathic alternatives to immunisation, it is usually an anxious time for parents as they seek reassurance that they are doing the right thing by having their child immunised. Parents have the difficult task of making an informed choice. Any doubts or questions that parents have about immunisation that parents address to you must be referred to their health visitor, practice nurse or GP. Urgent medical attention must be sought immediately if the child displays any of the following signs and symptoms:

SIGNS AND SYMPTOMS OF MENINGITIS

In babies:

▶ refusing to feed;
▶ high pitched moaning cry;

▶ drowsy, difficult to wake up;
▶ pale blotchy skin;
▶ red or purple spots that do not fade under pressure.

In children:

▶ a severe headache;
▶ dislike of bright lights;
▶ drowsiness or confusion;
▶ neck stiffness;
▶ red or purple spots that do not fade under pressure.

Recommended immunisation programme

According to the immunisation programme recommended by the Medical Research Council children should have received the following by:

▶ 6 months   3 doses of Diphtheria/Tetanus/Pertussis (DTP), Hib and Polio
▶ 15 months   first dose of Measles/Mumps/Rubella (MMR)
▶ school entry   second dose MMR, booster DTP and Polio

Communicable disease

As a carer manager you are responsible for the health and safety of the children in your setting during the day. Children must be capable of participating in the programme.

The following signs indicate communicable disease:

▶ Diarrhoea
▶ fever (temperature over 37.5°C)
▶ continuous vomiting
▶ Rash
▶ intense headache
▶ unusual drowsiness
▶ Red, running eyes
▶ earache
▶ productive coughs.

To maintain Health and Safety standards you should have a published policy on exclusion for childhood infections. Andreski and Nicholls (1996) recommend the following as a guide.

Guide to exclusion periods relating to childhood illnesses

Illness and incubation period (days)	Periods when infectious	Minimum period of exclusion
Chickenpox 11–21	1 day before to 6 days after appearance of rash	6 days from onset of rash
Rubella (German Measles) 14–21	few days before to 4 days after onset of rash	4 days from onset of rash (avoid contact or warn mothers who are under 14 weeks pregnant)
Measles 10–15	few days before to subsidence of rash	7 days from onset of rash
Mumps 12–26 (commonly 18)	few days before to 5 days after onset of swelling	until swelling has gone
Whooping cough (pertussis)	from 7 days after exposure to 21 days after onset of paroxysmal cough	21 days from onset of paroxysmal cough

Safety policies

Safety is a basic need for child and adult. Maslow classified the need for safety as the second most important need after physiological needs (see page 50). A safe environment is one in which the child or adult has a low risk of becoming ill or injured. The child's safety has to be incorporated in all aspects of their care and therefore requires provision and maintenance of an environment that is as safe as possible.

Manager's responsibilities

The safety of all children is of vital importance. To ensure the safety of children and adults, the manager will ensure that:

▶ A register of attendance is completed for each session and kept in known place.
▶ All children are supervised at all times. At least two adults will be present.
▶ An accident book is available for the reporting of incidents.
▶ All staff are aware of the security procedures for children's arrival and departure.
▶ Children will only be allowed home with a parent or authorised adult.
▶ Safety checks on premises in and outdoors are made as a daily routine measure.

- The perimeter of outdoor space will be securely fenced.
- In addition to weekly checks of equipment, any dangerous or faulty item noted will be discarded.
- Fire officer will be invited to keep a regular check on the premises.
- Fire drills will be held at least twice per term.
- All harmful substances including medicines must be appropriately stored.
- Children will only be allowed access to the kitchen area when accompanied by adults.
- A no smoking policy on the premises will be maintained for staff as well as visitors.
- All staff will complete a basic first aid course.
- The named first aider will take responsibility for keeping a well stocked first aid box.
- Adults will not walk around with hot drinks or leave them within reach of children.
- Prior to outings, consent will be obtained from parents.
- The adult:child ratio for outings will be one adult to two children.

The Health and Safety at Work Act 1974 (HASAW)

This Act brings together a range of legislation dating back to 1802. With the exception of domestic employment and the armed forces, the Act covers almost everyone in a work situation. The legislation protects not only people at work, but also the health and safety of the general public who may be affected by work activities. The Act places most of the responsibility for health and safety on the employer, although the legislation emphasises how important it is that everyone plays a part in health and safety.

Responsibilities under the Act are taken as what is 'reasonably practicable'. Within the remit then, employers must 'inform, instruct, train and supervise on all matters outlined in the Act and there should be a named person in the organisation with specific responsibility for Health and Safety'.

As a carer manager your responsibility is to ensure that:

- the nursery or playgroup environment and the materials and equipment are in a safe condition and present no risk to health;
- the handling, storage and transporting of substances and articles present no risk to health;
- there is provision of adequate first aid facilities and a safe working environment;

▶ there is provision of information, instruction training and supervision of all staff.

The legislation also requires employees to have a duty to:

▶ cooperate with you to ensure that the legal duty on health and safety is carried out;
▶ take reasonable care for the health and safety of themselves and others who may be affected by their actions i.e. colleagues, children, parents, people who may visit – health visitors etc;
▶ not intentionally or recklessly interfere with or misuse anything provided in the interest of health and safety and welfare: for example, allowing the children to play with the fire blanket.

As a carer manager or the **named person responsible for health and safety** you should be able to:

▶ keep yourself abreast of the current practices: e.g. read the relevant books and documents, seek out training as necessary;
▶ respond to situations of accident and emergency within the setting;
▶ plan and run activities safely, carry out regular risk assessments (see below);
▶ ensure the security of the staff and children within the setting at all times – this may involve installing a controlled entry system;
▶ ensure that a health and safety policy is drawn up, agreed and circulated to staff and parents.

Risk assessments

The Health and Safety at Work Act 1974 is supported by other regulations such as the Control of Substances Hazardous to Health (COSHH). As a regulatory body COSHH requires employers to complete a **risk assessment** of all hazardous substances used in the workplace. It defines 'hazard' as anything with the potential to cause harm and 'risk' as the likelihood that the hazard will cause harm.

To follow the guidelines, as a carer manager you will have to:

▶ identify any hazardous substance that is used e.g. bleach;
▶ identify who is at risk by specifying who uses the substance;
▶ evaluate the risk of a potential accident by assessing how it might cause damage to health and the seriousness of a likely accident;
▶ decide on control measures e.g. strict controls for use;
▶ record all assessments;
▶ review assessment regularly and additionally when there is a change of staff or purchase of new equipment.

Five steps to health and safety management

Under the Health and Safety at Work Act 1974, employers can be prosecuted, fined or imprisoned if representatives either of the two main bodies that enforce the law (i.e. Environmental Health Officers and Health and Safety Executives) inspect the setting and find the law disregarded or broken. The Health and Safety Executive recommend five steps to successful health and safety management:

1 Set your policy   PLANNING
2 Organise your staff   ORGANISING
3 Plan and set standards   LEADING
4 Measure performance   CONTROLLING
5 Audit and review   REVIEW

Ask yourself:

▶ Do you have a clear written policy for health and safety?
▶ Does the policy specify who has responsibility for identifying hazards, assessing and controlling risks?
▶ Do your staff have knowledge and understanding of the policy?
▶ Is the policy up to date?
▶ Does it prevent injuries, reduce losses and really affect the way you work?

The Food Safety Act 1990

Clear procedures should be drawn up for the preparation of food in line with the Act. The procedures must clearly state whose responsibility it is to cook the food. If the food has to be brought in from outside, great care must be taken with storage facilities.

Policy development

Policies are developed as guidelines for good practice. The Children Act 1989 specifies that in child care there should be policies related to the areas of Health and Safety. Behaviour Management, Equal Opportunities, Admission, Special Educational Needs, Confidentiality, Child Protection and Complaints Procedure.

The basis for a child care policy

If children are to be put first, their interest will need to be recognised at national, regional and local levels and represented by people capable of foreseeing and overseeing policy impacts on children and of highlighting and communicating trade offs.

(Penelope Leach, 1994)

Children are people. They are not inferior adults. Children have the right to special consideration from society because of their size and vulnerability. As 'apprentices in the business of growing up' (Leach) they need protection, nurturing and informed adults to teach them.

General policy

The first step in the strategic planning process is to identify and examine the mission statement of the child care centre.

The key characteristics of a good mission statement are

- ▶ **it must state in clear terms the purpose of the organisation;**
- ▶ **it must show concern for the welfare of the individual, parent and child.**

Therefore a child care mission statement might read:

'Our mission is to provide care and learning for any child, physically, emotionally and intellectually in line with their family's and society's needs and the law.'

This statement immediately provides the framework of the child care policy which defines the resources and practices required for safety, hygiene, nutrition, health, education and play.

Formulating a child care policy

A child care policy must be localised and tailored to the individual care centre. It must reflect the mission statement. The policy statement should be drawn up in consultation with a group representing the interests of the child, the parents or carers, the staff and the wider community.

Child protection

The Children Act 1989 defines harm as 'the significant ill-treatment or impairment of health and development' (to include intellectual, physical or behavioural). The Act does not define the word 'significant' but would compare the care given by a 'reasonable' adult to that which the child is receiving.

To promote a psychologically safe, caring environment it is your duty as a carer manager to be aware of, and have clear procedures to deal with, the very sensitive and highly emotive issue of child abuse. In a playgroup, day centre or nursery setting you must appoint a Child Protection Officer (CPO) who is aware of the procedures. All staff must be aware of the local authority guidelines. Child abuse represents a failure to respect the needs and rights of children. The following categories, from the Department of Health, are regarded as a guide to identification in cases where registration of abuse may be required.

Definitions of abuse

EMOTIONAL ABUSE

This occurs when a child consistently faces ill-treatment: verbal abuse, mocking, shouting. This may result in loss of self-esteem and confidence. The child may appear withdrawn, shy, apathetic and in some instances may display aggressive behaviour.

NEGLECT

Neglect occurs when the child is deprived of the essential physiological and safety needs: food, warmth, shelter and protection. Children thus abused present with eating and nutritional problems. Their growth and weight may be arrested and they can be admitted to hospital with a diagnosis of 'failure to thrive'.

PHYSICAL INJURY

Such injury occurs when a child is physically hurt or there is failure to prevent physical injury. Injuries include: bruising, bite marks, burns and scalds, fractures with no direct accidental history, haemorrhage which may be the result of shaking, squeezing, kicking or punching.

SEXUAL ABUSE

Sexual abuse occurs when dependent or developmentally immature children are coerced into sexual activities such as fondling or masturbation, which they do not understand or to which they are unable to consent. Children who have been affected may become withdrawn and depressed. They are more likely to minimise their violations than exaggerate their plight. There are physical factors such as soreness in the genital area, as well as inappropriate sexual behaviour.

Dealing with child abuse

The Children Act 1989 sets out a number of principles regarding the care of children and it is these principles that must guide and inform your practice. The key principles are:

▶ The welfare of the child is paramount.
▶ The wishes and feelings of children must be ascertained in light of their age and understanding.
▶ The rights of parents and children must be protected.
▶ The child's physical, emotional and educational needs must be respected.
▶ The child's age, sex, background and other relevant aspects must be respected.

The NSPCC (1994) reported that child abuse usually comes to the attention of teachers, staff or helpers in one or more of four ways:

▶ Directly from the child who has been abused;
▶ a third party report (e.g. a friend, or other child or relative);
▶ through the child's behaviour;
▶ your own observation of an injury to the child.

Reporting child abuse

Where child abuse is suspected, disclosed or the child presents with a non-accidental injury (NAI), the situation must be taken seriously and not trivialised. The child needs to know that they are believed and respected. Use open ended questions. Avoid pushing the child in specific directions. You might ask an encouraging question that partly repeats what the child has said and add on a more specific question. For example if the child says:

'My brother is mean to me.'
Your question might be: 'Mean, but how is he mean?'

You might follow this up with a simple open ended question. For example:

'Yes?' or 'What else happened?'

You must listen to the child's version of how they are feeling rather than making assumptions about their emotional state.

In the case of a childminder, where you are alone in suspecting the problem, it is good policy to voice your anxiety, and perhaps leave the interviewing to a social worker. In particular if sexual abuse has been disclosed, carers must ensure that any questioning is not prolonged and probing; the child will withdraw as a result of this form of interrogation. It is necessary to recognise the child's need for space. The incident must be reported immediately to Social Services and written records must be kept of all communication. The child should be kept informed, at their level of understanding, of what will happen next.

What is likely to happen next is a child protection investigation carried out by the police and social services working together. This is a statutory requirement. The investigating agency will interview the child, the designated CPO, parent and carer.

Parents must be involved as soon as possible. Most abused children return to living with their parents at home with support from child care agencies. There may be a medical examination. If concerns are sufficient there will be a child protection conference to decide if the child is likely to suffer further harm. If this is the case, the child's name will be placed on the Child Protection Register.

The Child Protection Register

In each Local Authority, Social Services produce a register that lists children, reported to have suffered a non-accidental injury or who are thought to be at risk of abuse. It is a record of unresolved child protection issues. The register exists for the protection of children, as those on the register are subject to a Child Protection Plan.

The Register acts as a child protection tool as it:

▶ Provides a record on a child who has been the victim of abuse or where concern has been expressed of suspected abuse.
▶ Allows you as a carer manager to telephone the Social Services Department to check whether a child about whom you are concerned is on the register.
▶ Provides information regarding the key worker taking responsibility for the child.
▶ Focuses the attention of those concerned on what might otherwise seem to be unrelated occurrences.
▶ Puts into action a Child Protection Plan that is reviewed every six months by agencies concerned.

CHILD PROTECTION PLAN

The Child Protection Plan is a plan devised by the local Social Services team to meet the needs of the individual child in question. The plan is crucial in helping to protect children. The plan sets out:

▶ an assessment in full of the child's situation;
▶ specific work to be done;
▶ the key tasks agreed as necessary to protect the child;
▶ what help the family concerned will be given;
▶ which agency will take on particular aspects of work;
▶ how often the agency workers will visit to check on the child's welfare;
▶ the name of the child's key worker.

All plans are reviewed every six months or earlier as appropriate. These provide an immediate assessment of the current situation and whether further intervention is required.

Child protection policy

EMPLOYMENT OF STAFF

▶ All applicants for employment at the setting will be interviewed before an appointment is made and will be asked to provide two consecutive references which will be followed up. It will be made clear that the position is exempt from the provisions of the Rehabilitation of Offenders Act 1974. Appointments are subject to a probationary period of one month.

STAFF TRAINING

▶ Training opportunities will be made available for staff to ensure that they recognise the symptoms of possible physical abuse, neglect, emotional abuse and sexual abuse.

GOOD PRACTICE

▶ Adults will not be left alone for long periods with individual children. An adult who needs to take a child aside will leave the door ajar.

LAYOUT OF ROOMS

▶ This will permit constant supervision of all children.
▶ 'Day care providers in the private and voluntary sector must have agreed procedures for contacting Local Authority Social Services about an individual child': (Children Act 1989). We are required by law to:

Respond appropriately to suspicions of abuse

▶ Changes in children's behaviour, physical condition or appearance noticed by carers will be discussed with parents.

▶ Suspicions of child abuse will also be referred as appropriate to local Social Services Department for further action.

▶ All suspicions and investigations will be kept confidential.

Keep records

▶ Carers will keep accurate, objective records of any incidents disclosures or observations at the time they occur. These will be kept confidential.

Liaise with other bodies

▶ The setting must operate in accordance with local authority guidelines.

▶ Confidential records kept on children about whom the setting is anxious will be shared with the local Social Services Department where it is felt that further action is needed.

▶ If a report on a child is to be made to the authorities, the child's parents will be kept informed at the same time as the report is made.

Support for families

▶ A policy of building up trust and supportive relationships between families and staff will be maintained.

▶ Where abuse at home is suspected, the setting will continue to welcome the child and family while investigations proceed.

▶ Confidential records kept on a child will be shared with the child's parents.

ACTIVITIES

After reading this chapter you may like to complete some of the following activities.

1. What measures would you take to maintain a healthy atmosphere for children? For example, consider the issues of:

▶ illness and incubation;
▶ immunisation;
▶ minimum periods of exclusion;
▶ first aid facilities and policy.

2. Which aspects of the Health and Safety at Work Act are applicable to your setting?

3. In case of suspected child abuse, what are the procedures of your setting?

4. FROM YOUR KNOWLEDGE OF SAFE FOOD PREPARATION, DRAW UP GUIDELINES WHICH ARE SPECIFIC TO YOUR SETTING.

5. DESIGN A CHILD PROTECTION PROCEDURES MANUAL FOR YOUR SETTING.

▶ Do you already have a system for recording information?
▶ Do all your staff know about the procedures?
▶ Do you already have a system for recording information?
▶ Have all your staff read the local authority procedures?
▶ Do you have a designated person for child protection?

References

Andreski R. and Nicholls, S. (1996) ‘*Managing Your Nursery*’. Nursery World: London.

Leach, P. (1994) *Children First*. London: Penguin Books.

NSPCC (1977) *Protecting children from Sexual Abuse in The Community: a guide for Parents and Carers*. London: NSPCC.

NSPCC (1994) *The Abuse of Children in Day Care Settings. Conference Report of June 1994*. London: NSPCC National Training Centre.

Further reading

Lindon, J. (1998) *Child Protection and Early Years Work*. London: Hodder & Stoughton.

Appendix

Relating modules/units of courses in Early Years Care and Education to chapters in the text.

Chapter Number and Title	NNEB Diploma Modules	NVQ Level 3 Early Years Care	ADCE Modules
1. Child Care in Perspective	Q		10
2. Models of Management		M2, P5	12
3. Managing Children's needs	Cii, F, H, J,	C5, C14	3
4. Managing the Environment	N	C10, C15	14
5. Managing an Early Years Curriculum	U	C11, C18, C24, C25	1, 5, 6
6. Managing the Challenging Child	J	C7, C16	9
7. Managing the Carers	P	MCI/CI	13
8. Managing Change	P	MCI/C4	9
9. Managing the Inspection Process	S	P8	23
10. Managing Health & Welfare	G	M20, M6	

Business Plan

If you need to seek a loan to start your nursery or playgroup, or improve your current accommodation, your bank manager will look more favourably on the project if you can present a coherent business plan. It is important to realise that the larger the sum of money required, the more elaborate and detailed the plan will have to be. The following is a guide to what the plan should cover.

Activity	Possible length
1 **Summary** Brief introduction as to: ▶ nature of the setting e.g. playgroup, nursery, home? ▶ what is the market e.g. 0–2 yrs, 0–4 yrs, 2–8 yrs? ▶ potential for business ▶ projected income ▶ amount of money needed	one–two pages
2 **History** ▶ when business started ▶ what is the financial health of the business ▶ state how relevant or not past performance is to future progress	one page with appendix showing finances
3 **Management** As the potential manager you will need to show: ▶ your employment history and business data ▶ highlight your achievements where applicable ▶ if not the sole carer, record of other staff	one page
4 **The market** ▶ give a clear description of the nature of the setting ▶ its size and future growth ▶ an analysis of who is likely to use your setting e.g. single parents ▶ your competitors – is there other provision nearby? ▶ are they over subscribed? ▶ will they welcome more child care provision?	two pages

5	**Advertising**	one page
▶	how are you going to promote your provision?	
▶	how will you make a difference?	
▶	how will you set your fees?	

6	**Operational details**	one page with appendix
▶	where will your provision be located?	of basic equipment
▶	how many staff will you require?	
▶	the equipment needed	

7	**Financial analysis**	one page plus
▶	summary of the forecasts	appendix of figures
▶	monthly profit and loss for a minimum of two years	
▶	monthly cash flow forecast for a minimum of two years	
▶	forecast balance sheet for a minimum of two years	
▶	give assumptions behind forecasts	
▶	give principal risks that could affect the figures e.g. number of young families leaving the area	

8	**The prospects**	one page
▶	your short term and long term objectives for a minimum of two years	
▶	the capital sum needed and what it is needed for	

Essential Policies

Equal Opportunities Policy

We aim to:

▶ acknowledge and value equally each child's individual stage, culture, religion, language, racial background and family group;
▶ actively seek to combat sexism and promote equal opportunities for girls and boys, women and men;
▶ encourage equality of opportunity for children with special needs and their families.

To achieve the above we will:

▶ plan our programme to extend the children's experience and knowledge of other cultures, languages and celebrations;
▶ ensure that the activities reflect the diversity of our society, not just our group;
▶ encourage children to explore in a positive way the differences and diversity of people, ensuring that representations of people are accurate and realistic;
▶ positively challenge stereotypes and assumptions – racist, sexist or concerning disabilities;
▶ enable adults with disabilities to take part in our group where it is safe and reasonable to so do.

Behaviour Management Policy

We aim to provide a stimulating environment in which children develop self-discipline and self-esteem.

▶ Clear, consistent boundaries are set regarding behaviour, taking into account the age and stage of development of the child.
▶ Positive methods of guidance are used. We reward good behaviour and encourage respect for others.
▶ Adults intervene and redirect, if necessary, to prevent disagreements developing that children cannot handle.
▶ Physical punishment is never used, nor are practices which humiliate or frighten children.
▶ Children who misbehave are given one-to-one adult support in analysing what went wrong and working towards more acceptable behaviour.
▶ It is always made clear that it is the behaviour, not the child, that is unwelcome.

Admissions Policy

We aim to make the group accessible to all families from the local community.

▶ We welcome fathers and mothers, other relatives, other carers and people from all cultural, ethnic, religious and social groups, with and without disabilities.

▶ We place notices advertising the group where all sections of the community can see them.

▶ Our waiting list is arranged in order of Date of Birth.

▶ In order to accommodate emergency admissions, we endeavour to keep a place vacant, if this is financially viable.

▶ We are flexible about attendance patterns in order to accommodate the needs of individual children and families.

▶ Two terms before a child is due to start at the group, we ask parents to pay a deposit to secure the child's place.

Settling-in Policy

If children are to play and learn successfully, they must feel secure and happy in the absence of their parents.

They need to be confident in the knowledge that their parents will return at the end of the session. In order to achieve these aims our policy is to:

▶ ask parents to visit;

▶ agree with parents how we will introduce and settle a child into the centre;

▶ ensure that the individual needs of the child and family are met;

▶ introduce children new to the centre in small numbers over a period of time;

▶ to give each child the adequate time and support needed to settle;

▶ encourage parents, where possible, to separate from their children for brief periods at first then gradually build up to longer absences;

▶ reassure parents who are anxious about their child by giving them information about their child's activities and welfare during the session;

▶ recall a parent if the child is distressed or unable to settle.

Special Educational Needs Policy

The aim of our group with regard to the DfEE Code of Practice on the Identification and Assessment of Special Educational Needs is to provide appropriate learning opportunities for all children.

▶ Children with special needs, like all children, are admitted to the group after consultation between parent and staff.

▶ Our system of observation and record keeping, which is shared with parents, enables us to monitor children's needs and progress on an individual basis.

▶ If it is felt that a child's needs cannot be met in the group without the support of a one-to-one relationship with an adult, funding will be sought to employ an extra member of staff.

▶ We work in liaison with professionals outside the group, including health visitors, therapists, psychologists, social workers and paediatricians to meet children's specific needs.

Our staff attend, wherever possible, training courses on Special Educational Needs arranged by Social Services and other professional bodies.

Bibliography and references

Alberdi de, L. (1990) *People Psychology and Business*. Cambridge: Cambridge University Press.

Allen, N. (1992) *Making Sense of the Children Act*. London: Longman Group.

Andreski, R. and Nichols, S. (1997) *Managing Children's Behaviour*. London: Nursery World.

Andreski, R. and Nichols, S. (1996) 'Managing Your Nursery' in *Nursery World*. London.

Are You Ready For Inspection? London: Office For Standards In Education.

Argyle, M. (1981) *The Psychology of Interpersonal Behaviour*. Harmondsworth: Penguin.

Axline, V. (1971) *Dibs: In Search of Self*. Harmondsworth: Penguin.

Axline, V. (1974) *Play Therapy*. Boston, Mass: Houghton Mifflin.

Barra, R. (1989) *Putting Quality Circles to Work*. New York: McGraw-Hill.

Bee, H. (1985) *The Developing Child*. New York: Harper & Row.

Berger, K. (1995) *The Developing Person and the Process of Parenting: Childhood and Adolescence*. New York: Werth.

Berne, E. (1966) in Pitman, E. (1984). *Transactional Analysis for Social Workers and Counsellors*. London: Routledge.

Bettleheim, B. (1987) *A Good Enough Parent*. London: Thames and Hudson.

Biddle, D. and Evenden, R. (1980) *Human Aspects of Management*. London: Institute of Personnel Management.

Bowlby, J. (1979) *The Making and Breaking of Affectionate Bonds*. London: Tavistock.

Brannen, J. and Moss, P. (1991) *Managing Mothers: Dual earner households after maternity leave*. London: Unwin Hyman.

Braun, D. 'Working with Parents' in Pugh, G. ed. (1992) *Contemporary Issues in the Early Years*. London: Paul Chapman Publishing.

Bray, M. (1989) *Children's Hour: A Special Listen*. Shrewsbury: Nightingale Books.

Breakwell, G.M. (1990) *Interviewing*. London: BPCC/Routledge.

Brooks, J. (1987) *The Process of Parenting*. London: Mayfield.

Bruce, T. (1996, 1987) *Early Childhood Education*. London: Hodder & Stoughton.

Bruce, T. (1991) *Time to Play*. London: Hodder & Stoughton.

Bruce, T. (1996) *Helping Young Children to Play*. London: Hodder & Stoughton.

Bruce, T. and Meggitt, C. (1996) *Child Care and Education*. London: Hodder & Stoughton.

Bruner, J. (1980) *Under Five in Britain: The Oxford Pre-School Project*. Oxford: Grant McIntyre/Blackwell.

Bryant, B., Harris, M. and Newton, D. (1980) *Children and Minders*. London: Grant McIntyre.

Bryant, B., Harris, M. and Newton, D. (1980) in Davenport, G.C. (1994) *An Introduction to Child Development*. London: Harper Collins.

Burningham, J. (1982) *Avocado Baby*. London: Picture Lions.

Carle, E. (1988) *The Very Busy Spider*. London: Hamish Hamilton.

Cattanch, A. (1988) *Protecting Children*. London: HMSO.

Cattanch, A. (1991) *Working Together Under the Children Act*. London: HMSO.

Cattanch, A. (1993) *Play Therapy with Abused Children*. London: Kingsley Ltd.

Cousins, J. (11 July 1996) 'Hidden Treasures' in *Nursery World*. London.

Cousins, J. (18 July 1996) 'A Whole New World' in *Nursery World*. London.

Culley, S. (1991) *Integrative Counselling Skills in Action*. London: Sage Publications Ltd.

Cunningham, C. and Davis, H. (1985) *Working with Parents*. London: Open University Press.

Curtis, A. (1998) *A Curriculum for the Pre-School Child*. London: Routledge.

Derman-Sparks, L. (1989) *The Anti-Bias Curriculum-Tools for Empowering Children*. National Association for the Education of Young Children.

DES (Rumbold Report) (1990) *Starting with Quality*. London: HMSO.

DfEE (1998) *Early Years Development Partnerships and Plans*. Sudbury: DfEE Publications Centre.

DfEE and SCAA (1996) *Nursery Education Scheme: The Next Steps*. Sudbury: DfEE Publications Centre.

DfEE and SCAA (1996) *Nursery Education: Desirable Outcomes for Children's Learning*. Sudbury: DfEE Publications Centre.

DfEE (1994) *Code of Practice on the Identification and Assessment of Special Educational Needs*. London: Central Office of Information, HMSO.

DfEE (1998) *Early Years Development Partnerships and Plans*. Sudbury: DfEE Publications Centre.

Drucker, P. (1954) *The Practice of Management*. New York: Harper.

Drucker, P. (1973) *People and Performance*. New York: Harper & Row.

Drummond, M.J., Rouse, D. and Pugh, G. (1992) *Making Assessment Work*. NES Arnold, National Children's Bureau.

Dunnell, K. (1976) *Family Formation Survey*. London: OPCS.

Elliott, M. (1994) *Keeping Safe: a Practical Guide to Talking with Children*. London: Hodder & Stoughton.

Erikson, E.H. (1972) *Play and Development*. New York: W.W. Norton.

Evans, D. (1986) *People, Communications and Organisations*. London: Pitman Publishing.

Evans, M. (1969) *Path Goal Theory*. New York: Random House.

Family Policy Bulletin. 1994, 1995, 1996, 1997. London: Family Policy Studies Centre.

Ferri, E. and Smith, K. (1996) *Parenting in the 1990s*. London: Family Policy Studies Centre.

Fielder, F.E. (1967) *A Theory of Leadership Effectiveness*. New York: McGraw-Hill.

Freud, S. (1936) *The Problem of Anxiety*. New York: W.W. Norton.

Freud, S. (1974) *Introductory Lectures on Psychoanalysis*. Harmondsworth: Penguin Books.

Garland, C. and White, S. (1980) *Children and Day Nurseries*. London: Grant McIntyre.

Garvey, C. (1997) *Play*. London: Fontana Open Books.

Gesell, A. and Ilg, F. (1946) *The Child from Five to Ten*. New York: Harper and Brothers.

Goldschmied, E. and Jackson, S. (1994) *People Under Three*. London: Routledge.

Gura, P. (1992) *Exploring Learning*. Paul Chapman Ltd.

Handy, C. (1996) *Understanding Organisations*. London: Penguin Books.

Hardy, M. et al. (1995) *Studying Child Psychology*. Oxford: Oxford University Press.

Hayward, S. (1996) *Applying Psychology To Organisations*. London: Hodder & Stoughton.

Herzberg, F. (1966) *Work and the Nature of Man*. Cleveland: World Publishing.

HMSO (1993) *General Household Survey*. 1991, 1992, 1994. London: HMSO.

Hobart, C. and Frankel, J. (1994) *Child Observation*. Cheltenham: Stanley Thornes.

Hoing, A. (1979) *Parent Involvement in Early Childhood Education*. Washington DC: National Association for the Education of Young Children.

Holman, M., Barnet, B. and Wickhart, D. (1979) *Young Children in Action*. London: High-Scope Press.

Hunt, J. (1981) *Managing People at Work*. London: Pan Books Ltd.

Ilg, F. and Bates, A. (1966) *The Gesell Institute's Child Behaviour*. New York: Harper & Row.

Isaacs, S. (1930) *Intellectual Growth in Young Children*. London: Routledge and Kegan Paul.

Isaacs, S. (1954) *The Educational Value of the Nursery School*. London: BAECE.

Joshi, H. (1989) *The Changing Population of Britain*. Oxford: Blackwell.

Katzenbach, J. and Smith, D. in Montebello, A.R. (1994) *Work Teams that Work*. New York: PHD Bestsellers Publishing Co.

Kellmer-Pringle, M. (1974) (1980 second edition) *The Needs of Children*. London: Hutchinson.

Kerr, S. ed. (1968) *Ultimate Rewards: What Really Motivates People to Achieve?* New York: Harvard Business School.

Kootz, H. 'Towards a Unified Theory of Management' in Eyre, E.C. (1982) *Mastering Basic Management*. London: Macmillan Press.

Lazarus, R. and Folkman, S. (1984) *Stress Appraisal and Coping*. New York: Springer Publication.

Leach, P. (1974) *Who Cares?* London: Penguin.

Leach, P. (1992) *Getting Positive About Discipline: a guide for today's parents*, and *Why speak out against smacking: questions and answers for the physical punishment debate*. Essex: Barnados.

Leach, P. (1994) *Children First*. London: Penguin Books.

Leach, P. (1997) *Young Children Under Stress* (National Early Years Network – Starting Points No. 6).

Lear, R. (1986) *Play Helps*. Oxford: Heinemann Medical Books.

Lewin, K. (1947) 'Group Decision and Social Change' in Newcombe, T. and Hartley, E. (1963) *Readings in Social Psychology*. New York: Holt, Reinhart and Winston.

Lewin, K., Lippett, R. and White, R.K. (1937) in Hayward, S. (1996) *Applying Psychology to Organisations*. London: Hodder & Stoughton.

Likert, R. (1961) *New Patterns of Management*. New York: McGraw-Hill.

Lindon, J. (1998) *Child Protection and Early Years Work*. London: Hodder & Stoughton.

Mayall, B. and Petrie, P. (1983) *Childminding and Day Nurseries: what kind of care?* London: Heinemann Educational Books.

Mckay, M., Davis, M. and Fanning, P. (1983) *Messages: The Communication Skills Book*. California: New Harbinger Publications.

Milar, S. (1968) *The Psychology of Play*. Harmondsworth: Penguin.

Miller, A. (1987) *The Drama of Being a Child*. London: Virago.

Miller, J. and Wiseman, S. (1986) *The Parent's Guide to Daycare*. London: Bantam.

Milne, A. A. (1989) *When We Were Very Young*. London: Methuen.

Montessori, M. (1949) *The Absorbent Mind*. Madras, Adyar: Theosophical Publishing House.

Montessori, M. (1912) *The Montessori Method*. London: Heinemann.

Newell, P. and Potts, P. (1984) *Under Fives with Special Needs*. London: Advisory Centre for Education.

Newell, P. (1991) *The United Nations Convention and Children's Rights in the UK*. London: National Children's Bureau.

NSPCC (1992) *Child Protection Procedures*. London: NSPCC.

NSPCC (1995) *The Abuse of Children in Day Care Settings: conference report of June 1994*. London: NSPCC National Training Centre.

NSPCC (1997) *Protecting Children from Sexual Abuse in the Community: a guide for parents and carers*. London: NSPCC.

NSPCC (1997) *Stop the Violence: a guide to keeping children safe*. London: NSPCC.

Ofshe, R. and Walters, E. (1995) *Making Monsters: False Memories Psychotherapy and Sexual Hysteria*. London: Andre Deutsch.

Paley, V. (1991) *The boy who would be a helicopter*. Cambridge, Mass.: Harvard University Press.

Peters, T. (1984) *In Search of Excellence*. New York: Harper & Row.

Piaget, J. (1948) *The Language and Thought of the Child*. London: Routledge and Kegan Paul.

Piaget, J. (1954) *The Origins of Intelligence*. London: Routledge and Kegan Paul.

Piaget, J. (1986) *Six Psychological Studies*. London: London University Press.

Porras, J. and Silvers, R.C. (1991) *Organisational Development and Transformation*. New York: American Review of Psychology, 42, 51–78.

Roberts, R. (1995) *Self Esteem and Early Successful Learning*. London: Hodder & Stoughton.

Robertson, J. and Robertson, J. (1967) *Young Children in Brief Separation: I, Kate Aged Two Years and Five Months in Foster Care for 27 Days*. London: Tavistock Child Development Research Unit.

Rodd, J. (1984) *Leadership in Early Childhood Services: the pathway to professionalism*. Buckingham: Open University Press.

Rogers, C. (1961) *On Becoming a Person*. Boston: Houghton Miflin.

Rogers, W. and Roche, J. (1994) *Children's Welfare and Children's Rights*. London: Hodder & Stoughton.

Rutter, M. (1972) *Maternal Deprivation Reassessed*. Harmondsworth: Penguin.

Rutter, M. (1992) *Developing Minds*. Harmondsworth: Penguin.

Salisbury, D.M. and Begg, N.T. ed. (1996) *Immunisation against Infectious Diseases*. London: HMSO.

SCAA (1997) *Looking at Children's Learning*. London: School Curriculum Assessment Authority.

Schaffer and Emmerson (1964) in Davenport, G.C. (1994) *An Introduction to Child Development*. London: Collins Educational.

Schaffer, H.R. (1977) *Mothering*. London: Fontana Open Books.

Siraj-Blackford, I. (1993) *The Early Years: laying the foundation for racial equality*. Stoke on Trent: Trentham Books.

Smith, D.R. (1993) *Safe from Harm: Code of Practice for Safeguarding the Welfare of Children in Voluntary Organisations in England in Wales*. London: Home Office.

Social Policy Research. 1995, 1996, 1997. London.

Social Policy Trends 28 (1988) London: Office for National Statistics.

Sylva, K., Roy, C. and Painter, M. (1980) *Child Watching at Playgroup and Nursery School*. London: Grant McIntyre.

Thornton, D. (September, 1997) 'All Our Children Are Special'. Seminar given at the Nursery World Early Years Conference, London.

Tobin, J. et al. (1989) *Pre-school in Three Cultures*. New Haven: Yale University Press.

Twigg, J. (1992) *Carer: Research and Practice*. London: HMSO.

Velez, G. (1986) *The Parent's Resources Book*. New York: New American Library.

Vernon, P.E. (1972) *Intelligence and Cultural Environment*. London: Methuen.

Vygotsky, L. (1978) *Mind in Society*. Cambridge, Mass.: Harvard University Press.

Ward, A. (1993) *Working in Group Care*. London: Venture Press.

Watson, J.B. (1928) *Psychological Care of Infant and Child*. New York: W.W. Norton.

Whalley, M. (1994) *Learning to Be Strong. Setting Up a Neighbourhood Service for Under Fives and their Families*. London: Hodder & Stoughton.

White, Carr and Lowe (1990) *A Guide to The Children's Act 1989*. London: Butterworths.

Williams, S. (1997) *Small Business Guide*. London: Penguin.

Willmott, P. (1986) *Social Networks, Informal Care and Public Policy*. London: Policy Studies Institute.

Winnicott, D. (1974) *Playing and Reality*. London: Pelican Books.

Yeoman, J. and Blake, Q. (1970) *The Bear's Water Picnic*. London: Macmillan.

Videos

1. BBC *Children without Prejudice* available from EYTARN, PO Box 28, Wallasey L45 9NP.
   Demonstrates how to implement the anti-racist and multicultural guidance of the Children Act. Shows how very young children acquire attitudes towards languages, cultures, skin colour. Suggests how those involved with young children can help them to view these differences positively.
2. BBC Educational Developments *Tuning into Children* available from PO Box 50, Weatherby, West Yorkshire LS23 7EX.
   A video and accompanying book by Tina Bruce about children's development and learning, useful when training and updating adult's.
3. BBC *Play for Asian Parents and Children* available from N. Films, 78 Holyhead Road, Birmingham B21 0LH.
   Shows the importance of play and the integral roles of language and culture in it. Stresses the need for bi-lingual children's books.
4. CCETSW *Awards 98* An introduction in the Revised Awards in Care and Early Years Care and Education available from Derbyshire House, St. Chad's Street, London WC1H 8AD.
   Explains the revises awards and the improved assesssment process.
5. Channel 4 (1995) *Baby Its You*.
   A useful video which follows individual children chronologically through stages in early development.
6. Davids, K. (1994) *Child Studies* available from Video Reportage Productions, 20 West Parade, Norwich NR2 2DW.
   Shows development stages and how family input influences a child's learning, language and attention span.
7. Davids, K. (1994) *Child Studies* available as above.
   Describes the psychology of play-peer interaction, language and social skills and looks at how the attitudes and behaviour of the pre-school are moulded by the values of the family.
8. Goldschmied, E. (1987) *Infants at Work* available from National Children's Bureau, 8 Wakely Street, London EC1V 7QE.
   Shows babies exploring a 'treasure basket' containing everyday objects which offer learning experiences through the six senses.
9. Golschmied, E. and Hughes, A. (1993) *Heuristic Play with Objects* available from Children's Bureau. 8 Wakely Street, London EC1V 7QE.
   Shows infants discovering for themselves how to use play materials, chosen to appeal to their innate curiosity.
10. RNIB *The World in our Hands* available from National Education Centre, Garrow House, 190 Kensal Road, London W10 5BT.
    Five videos about blind children.
11. The National Autistic Society (1994) *Behind the Invisible Wall* available from 393 City Road, London EC1V 1NE.
    Aimed at professionals, students and parents, this video describes Autism and provides examples of typical behaviour.

Index